HEY,
WE NEED TO
TALK

HEY, WE NEED TO TALK

CANDID CONVERSATIONS & DISCOVERIES FROM "THE MIDDLE"

JOSHUA D. BLOCKER

JuJo
PUBLISHING CO.

Copyright © 2025 by Joshua Blocker
All rights reserved. No part of this publication may be reproduced, stored in a retrieval system, or transmitted in any form or by any means—electronic, mechanical, photocopying, recording, or otherwise—without the prior written permission of the publisher, except for brief quotations used in reviews, commentary, or educational purposes.

First Edition

ISBN: 978-1-7375247-6-2

Library of Congress Control Number: 2025917251

Published by JuJo Publishing Co.

An imprint of DAWAY Entertainment

www.dawayent.com

Scripture Permissions:

Unless otherwise noted, all Scripture quotations are taken from the King James Version (KJV) of the Bible. Public domain.

Scripture quotations marked NLT are taken from the Holy Bible, New Living Translation, copyright © 1996, 2004, 2015 by Tyndale House Foundation. Used by permission of Tyndale House Publishers, Inc., Carol Stream, Illinois 60188. All rights reserved.

Scripture quotations marked NIV are taken from the Holy Bible, New International Version®, NIV®. Copyright © 1973, 1978, 1984, 2011 by Biblica, Inc.™ Used by permission. All rights reserved worldwide.

The "NIV" and "New International Version" trademarks are registered in the United States Patent and Trademark Office by Biblica, Inc.™

Dictionary References:

Select definitions and language explanations are drawn from public domain sources or referenced in accordance with fair use from Merriam-Webster's Collegiate Dictionary and similar reference works, for educational and commentary purposes.

This book is a work of nonfiction. All testimonies and stories are based on real experiences unless otherwise noted. Some names and identifying details may have been changed to honor privacy.

Printed in the United States of America

For speaking engagements, bulk orders, or more information, visit:

www.dawayent.com

"For those who've been on the brink of giving up when the road became too tough and answers seemed out of reach."

CONTENTS....

THIS IS US	10
THE INEVITABLE	20
HOW DID YOU GET HERE?	40
SAFE-ISH	58
THE FIGHT OF MY LIFE	78
DEAR GOD	88
WHAT'S THIS...WHO DAT?!	122
TAKEN	140
BLESSED RE-ASSURANCE	160
WHEN	182
FINAL THOUGHTS	202
ACKNOWLEDGMENTS	206
ABOUT THE AUTHOR	208

HEY, WE NEED TO TALK

"I DON'T LIKE WHERE I AM... I DON'T LIKE HOW I FEEL. WHO'S IN CHARGE HERE? GOD, I NEED YOU TO TAKE MY NAME OFF THAT 'STRONG SOLDIER' LIST OF YOURS. I'M TIIIIED"

INTRODUCTION

THIS IS US

> "LOOKING UNTO JESUS THE AUTHOR AND FINISHER OF OUR FAITH;..."
>
> HEBREWS 12:2A (KJV)

The middle is where life gets loud. It's where faith feels tested, where joy feels missing, and where God feels silent. But it's also where He does His best work. This book is my attempt to have a real conversation with you about surviving and discovering — the middle.

Do you remember sitting in front of your TV at home or going to the movies, being so captivated by a film or show that you didn't want to blink? I certainly do. I often tell people that the shows I rewatch or binge and the films I rave about captivate me for reasons beyond what meets the eye. While most people love their favorite TV show or film because of a favorite actor or the suspense and drama, I'm different. I'm a storyteller.

To know me is to know that I act, write, direct, and more. For years, it was hard to describe myself because, although I act, I'm not just an actor—I do so many other things. I fell in love with calling myself a storyteller because it's the thread that ties all my creative endeavors together. When I watch something, I'm not just interested in the acting or the actors; I love to peel back the layers and discover the choices made.

Why start here? Why this time period? If you ever hear me rave about something I've watched, you'll hear me say, "I LOVE SMART WRITING" or "This is how it should be done."

As a storyteller, I fall in love with things like setting, plot, soundtrack, casting, and even conflict. These are the elements that make stories make sense. And for me, things have to make sense. Once things stop making sense, you lose me, because it reveals that something important was missed and nobody caught it. That carelessness bothers me so much that I become disinterested in what happens next. I'll pull out my soapbox and sound the alarms—that's how important storytelling is to me. As a writer, it's one of the main reasons I pace the floor, making sure I'm thorough. It's easy to get lazy and rush to the finish, resulting in a sloppy presentation, and I hate that.

One of my favorite shows of all time is the NBC hit *This Is Us*. When I tell you I love this show—believe me. It epitomizes what I mean by a show that captivated me from the start. I cried, yelled at the TV, live-tweeted, and never missed an episode. I behaved this way because, to me, this show was masterfully done. The writing, the intention, the performances, the directing—the storytelling was absolutely superb. Everything made sense; it was so smart that even when you thought there was a plot hole or had questions, by the end of the season, everything came together perfectly. I loved the foreshadowing, the flashbacks, the multiplicity of stories being told at once with little to no plot holes. After the show ended, I read an article where the creator revealed that he visualized the series finale during season one. This blew my mind but made sense to me. As an author of many books and scripts, one of my writing hacks is that I don't start writing until I can see the finish line. It helps me stay focused and build a road map to get there.

Even with my love for the entire series, after finishing the show, I went back and watched the series preview and became irate—not at the preview, but at its symbolism. The preview gives you this cheesy, seemingly happy story about a pregnant couple about to give birth to two of their three children, and it cuts to a fact about how 18 million people share the same birthday, showcasing a quest for family, love, support, and happiness. By the end of the trailer, you're filled with "ooohs" and "ahhhs." But in reality, the show and the trailer are nothing alike. When I tell you that show took me through it, believe me—I still cry to this day about moments in the show that the trailer didn't reveal.

You have to understand—I loathe surprises. I'd rather you just give me the real spill upfront and let me choose to engage or not, rather than showing me something, getting my hopes up, and then delivering something completely different. Previews typically show beautiful beginnings and happy or resolute endings but tend to leave out what happens in the middle. This bothered me because it reminded me of how God speaks and reveals things. He speaks in previews or parts, as the Bible says. Great, fine, and dandy, but it bothers me because why not just tell me everything upfront so I can at least brace myself for what's to come?

The Bible says that *His ways are not like ours and His thoughts are far from ours*, and boy, isn't that the truth. If I had it my way, there wouldn't be any elements of surprise; everything would be written out for proper execution. But God is not me. I have to remind myself of that often because it's easy to think you know what's best when, in reality, you don't. God will often show you or speak to the end of a thing and then leave the gap between promise and fulfillment for you to navigate through. You find yourself in constant transition, which often makes you question your existence. That's where I found myself — not at the beginning, not at the end, but stuck in the messy in-between. And if you've ever been there, you know exactly what I mean.

One day, during one of my many tantrums thrown toward heaven about where I am, why I'm there, and how long I feel

I've been there, I got a revelation about why God doesn't provide the beginning, middle, and end. Hebrews 12:2 states, *"Looking unto Jesus, the author and finisher of our faith..."* It became very clear to me that the middle was never His responsibility. His role as author hit me deeply because I, too, am an author—not on His level, but an author nonetheless. You're not just an author because you put words to paper and produce a book; you're an author because you are an originator. You invent worlds, people, or characters. You create a story for them—a chain of events that propels them toward the end, with no rubric or example. But as the author, you know your intention towards them, and it's never to hurt them. Sometimes, pain and conflict are the only ways to cause progression.

    I have a book series titled *Sins of a Mother* that follows the life of a battered girl thrown into a series of tumultuous events, resulting in her becoming a teenage mother and ultimately a heartbroken and damaged adult mother. In reviewing the series of books I wrote, not once did I sit down and say, "I want Tarrylyn to have the most difficult life one could ever have." No, I wrote the initial book to save lives and push an agenda of truth, because you don't know how a simple lie might ruin the lives of people you claim to love. Tarrylyn goes from one situation to the next, overcoming one thing only to be overtaken by the next. Is it painful? Yes. At times, there is pleasure, laughter, and love, but it's easy to deduce that Tarrylyn has a hard life. However, the life I intend for her is one that is beautiful, most cherished, and appreciated. As the author, you see the whole picture. As characters, we can only see where we are now, and this creates conflict when the character tries to assume the role of author. They don't know how to guide themselves to the expected end because they aren't privy to the information the author holds. I know your chest got tight reading that, but it's the truth nonetheless. God is the originator of all this, and only He knows in full strength and detail why you were created and the intended impact of your existence. Only He knows how all this wraps up because He is both Originator and Finisher. Just like the creator of *This Is Us,* He saw the end from the beginning, and it's our job to play our role and reach the expected end. My favorite part about that "Finisher" word is that it means perfecter. It's His job to tie up loose ends, to place you in the positions and spaces that lead you to your end. He is also the editor—He can add and erase as He pleases. He is sovereign and can do what He wants, but you have to remember that He has no ill intent towards you. There are things that my characters learn by navigating the middle that they would never have gotten had I just taken them from start to finish. There is a process that we all must go through, and that process is called the middle. The middle comes with a lot of surprises, tears, wins, losses, disappointments, and more, but all of it works for good, ultimately shaping them into their intended impact.

The middle is *GHETTO!* Trust me, I know firsthand, which is why I'm penning this book now. My aim here is simply to relate to you, to disarm you from thinking that this is an isolated event for you. This is not advice from the other side of things. This is me, right here in the waiting room of life being processed and searched, with you! Much like Joseph, I've seen the end, and it's great, but what I need help with is navigating the hurt, the disappointment, the betrayal, and the setbacks that lead to the palace or place of promise.

One Saturday morning, June 18th, 2022, to be exact, I was lying in bed, depressed and unmotivated to do anything because life felt unfair. And if I'm honest, which I intend to be throughout this book, life still feels unfair. But God came into my room and ministered to my spirit. He shared some things with me and opened my eyes to what was to come. He said to me that day, *"Meet me on the other side."* In the middle, it's easy to lose hope; one of the things you feel like doing most is giving up and throwing in the towel. But I'm here to remind you that there is another side to all of this, and it's beautiful—you've just got to stay the course and trust Him as the author and finisher.

I've included my deeply personal journal entries because I never want you to invalidate your feelings. Your emotions are real, but they are not always the truth. And yes—you should absolutely feel them. This is your permission to be unfiltered, to un-sanitize your emotions, because God can handle your raw, unprocessed feelings.

This book is born from countless heart-to-heart conversations I've had with God. Here's what I've learned: the key to meaningful conversation is confrontation. In these pages, you'll see my confrontations, contradictions, and confirmations. You'll witness my struggle as I wrestle with what I feel versus what I know, and what I see compared to what I believe.

The stories, journal entries, revelations, and discoveries shared here are meant to provide insight that encourages you to shift your perspective—not necessarily to mine, but to one you may not have considered before. My prayer is that this book gives you hope, uplifts you, and equips you with tangible tools to navigate the challenging space called the middle.

So here's my ask: don't just read this book. Talk back to it. Question it. Argue with it if you need to. Because this isn't just my conversation — it's ours. Welcome to the middle.

"THE WRITER'S ROOM OF MY LIFE IS GOING CRAZY... EVERYDAY FEELS LIKE THE SEASON FINALE.. MY LIFE FEELS LIKE A COURTNEY KEMP AND SHONDA RHYMES COLLAB. PUT THE PEN DOWN!"

HEY GOD,
WHAT IS HAPPENING ?!?!

Today, I feel incredibly discouraged... I'm completely out of sync.

I went to Popeyes, and something as simple as them not having dark meat almost brought me to tears. It feels like nothing is going right—everything is a "no," everything is difficult. Lord, is there something I'm doing that's making my life so hard right now? I feel so defeated because the more I try to get things in order, the harder everything seems to become. I'm overwhelmed and on the verge of breaking... It feels like things keep going wrong, and I've been struggling for so long. Please, just some relief—please.

I'm trying to stay grateful and even force a smile, but it's tough. Every day is a reminder of what I don't have, and I'm doing my best not to sink into despair. I wonder how everyone else seems to walk around with so much joy, as if nothing is wrong.

What am I supposed to do? If I stop caring, it's bad, but if I care, I worry. I'm lost... I feel so much pressure that I think I might burst.

1.
THE INEVITABLE

I grew up in an old-school Pentecostal church. The foundation of my faith and relationship with God was built in a beautiful brick building on the corner of Fordham and S. Lancaster Road in Oak Cliff, Texas—Bethel Temple Pentecostal Church. I saw and learned so much in that church, things I still treasure to this day. I could tell you countless stories—some encouraging, some hilarious, some painful—but all unforgettable.

One of my favorite parts of growing up in that church was something we called "Testimony Service." It was a segment in the service where members of the congregation could stand and tell of the goodness of God, often as a way to uplift someone else. You could speak or sing—some did both—and I especially loved those bold enough to sing their testimony.

One of those people was my aunt, who also served as the First Lady of our congregation. When she stood up, she could command the entire room. Her favorite song to sing was "Hold to God's Unchanging Hand." I loved when she sang it—not just because of the melody, but because of the energy and authority she brought. With a charismatic charge, she'd belt, "Everybody ought to hold to His hand—God's unchanging hand!" I fell in love with the song as a child and teenager because of how she delivered it. But I didn't fully grasp the weight of its message until much later.

The song speaks of life's many inconsistencies and changes, but it offers one unshakable hope: God's hand doesn't change. The first line says, "Time is filled with swift transition," and my God—did I come to know the truth of that line for myself. You might put it like this: "If it ain't one thing, it's another." The painful reality of life is that nothing stays the same. Every day we're confronted with change we didn't ask for. Plans get derailed. Exits get missed. People we thought were solid crumble—and it hurts. There's no time to brace for impact. One minute everything is fine; the next, what was is no more. And the pain that brings is often both unimaginable and unbearable.

The past few years of my life have been painfully tough. If I had to mark a starting point, I'd say May of 2022. That's when things really started to get ghetto. I didn't realize it at the time, but these moments became the picture of what the middle feels like — ordinary one second, overwhelming the next.

Mother's Day fell on a Sunday that year, and after service, I received a call urging me to get to the hospital—my grandmother had been admitted. We found out she had stage 4 cancer, but we weren't alarmed. Granny was a fighter. When I got to the hospital, she smiled and told us everything would be fine. I remember saying, "Alright now, Sadie Ann, take it easy. You've got great-grandchildren to meet."

At the same time, I was dealing with a toxic, high-stress work environment. And just a few weeks later, I got another call—my cousin had passed away. I was devastated. Yes, she had been sick, but I was believing God for healing. I was heartbroken. Naturally, I don't handle death well—it takes me time to process and accept it. I wrestled with it hard. My faith took a hit.

Ironically, I was preaching heavily during this time. That's the hard tension—preaching faith while quietly losing your own. I remember preaching a message called *Cancel the Funeral* the Sunday after her services. I walked through Paul's shipwreck and snake bite—how he survived what should've killed him. I said in that sermon that shipwreck was coming, and boy, did it come. I didn't know I was entering a season of constant loss and instability. Every other week, it felt like someone else had died. Friends, distant relatives... it just kept happening.

But the loss that hit hardest was my grandmother.

On July 15, 2022, I was working a normal shift, counting down the hours until I could head to a birthday party that night. The day was going fine until I checked my phone and saw a message from my eldest cousin: "Drop what you're doing. Get to the hospital. Granny's throwing up blood."

I immediately got permission to leave work and rushed over. I hate hospitals, outside of births, nothing good usually happens there. When I arrived, my family was already in the waiting room. My mind started racing—I'm a chronic overthinker. I tried to stay calm, but it was hard. I like to joke that I'm a doctor because I've seen every season of Grey's Anatomy (multiple times). But even in a TV show, throwing up blood is never a good sign.

Finally, around 7 PM, a nurse came out. We all jumped up. She told us they had located the cause of bleeding, stopped it, and got my grandmother settled into a recovery room. Relief swept over the room. The panic didn't vanish, but hope returned.

I ended up going to my friend's party after all, hoping it would distract me. I was still fragile inside, but grateful. I thought everything was going to be fine. I had a pool party planned the next day and convinced myself that my Grandma just needed rest.

But the next day came, and she still hadn't woken up. The doctors told us it wasn't unusual—she'd lost a lot of blood. Still, it unsettled me. My aunt called an emergency family meeting. It felt like that Soul Food scene where Ahmad tries to keep the family together. I felt like Ahmad.

The topic of life support came up. I got emotional and said, "Yeah, we don't want her to suffer—but we're giving her every fighting chance."

Even after the meeting, she still wasn't awake. Sunday morning came and I went to church as usual. Just before service, my phone rang again—another high-stress call. Fear overtook me in the hallway. A fellow minister hugged me and prayed over me. I called my sister and, through tears, she told me our Grandma had woken up and was asking for her children and grandchildren. Relief. And slight irritation. "Lead with that next time," I said.

I arrived at the hospital, walked into her room, and saw her talking to my sister. When she saw me, she called me by my nickname—"Come here, Grandpa." She reached for me and pulled me into a hug. But it wasn't just a hug—it was the hug. The kind that says, "This is the last one." I refused to believe it but couldn't deny what I'd felt.

More family arrived. I tried to shake off the feeling, but I couldn't. When the nurse came in, I started asking questions. She gave us a two-week timeline, saying not to be alarmed if blood showed up in bowel movements. She said it was normal. Everyone else felt better. I didn't.

My grandma saw me sitting quietly. She called me over again and started kissing my forehead and cheeks. Over and over, she whispered, "I love you." Something deep inside told me—this was the beginning of the end.

We left that night. I drove home. My comfort shows are Toy Story or Barney—don't judge me. I put on Toy Story. Just as Woody made his entrance, my aunt FaceTimed all the grandkids. Her face said it all.

"Call off work tomorrow," she said. "Things took a turn. The doctors said there's nothing more they can do. We're moving her into hospice."

I lost it.

How did we go from "she's recovering" to hospice in a matter of an hour? I asked all the right questions. How did we get here?

It was Monday. We were back at the hospital. The atmosphere was bleak and somber. Everyone was trying to stay in good spirits, but how could we? Our grandmother—our matriarch—was being moved to the hospice wing. The place where comfort takes precedence over cure. None of us could fully process it.

A hospital chaplain came in and asked who would like to lead the prayer. My mother and I were the only ordained clergy in the room, and neither of us could find the strength. I tried. I really did. I opened my mouth to say "Father..." but before I could finish, my grandmother sat up in the bed and led her own prayer:

"Lord, we thank You for this day. We thank You that no weapon formed against us shall prosper. We thank You that by Your stripes we are healed. We are in Your blood. And whatever You have to say about it—we say Yes, Lord."

On her deathbed, my grandmother still had a "Yes, Lord." A yes that would ultimately mean her transition out of this life, but a yes nonetheless.

When people ask me about it, I often say that her passing was the fastest-slowest transition I've ever experienced. It was torture. Over the span of nine days, I watched my grandmother slowly fade. I used to think that not being present—like when my big brother died in a motorcycle accident in 2011—was the worst kind of pain. But this... this was worse. Being there. Watching every moment. It shattered something inside of me.

I watched her eat her last full meal. I watched her shift to ice chips. I noticed when her kidneys stopped producing urine. I listened as she said her final words—calling out her sister's name. I remember walking in, checking her feet to see if they were warm. Holding her hand through every labored breath.

On the morning of July 26th, at 12:10 a.m., my grandmother took her last breath. I walked into the room and laid on her lifeless body until the staff came to move her to the morgue. That moment changed me forever.

Grief consumed me in a way I still can't articulate. I remember lying in the bathtub, crying—begging God to take my life too. My heart was that broken. I tried to go back to work, but the smallest things would undo me. Seeing flowers on my desk triggered a deep depression. I didn't want to get out of bed. I didn't want to eat. I didn't want to talk. I couldn't even name what I was feeling.

And just when I thought the losses were done—five months later, her oldest daughter, my aunt, passed away. Same hospital. Same tower. I watched my mother and surviving aunt morph into little girls again as they lost their sister, after just losing their mother.

One week later—another uncle passed.
The month after that—yet another.
Then, a classmate of mine died suddenly.
And the day after that, I walked into the job I had worked at for seven years. They called me into the conference room and said, "We've decided today will be your last day."
Blow after blow. Loss after loss. Adjustment after adjustment.
I became numb. I lost my will to live.
I almost came into agreement with death.
Because time really is filled with swift transition.

There are some people... some things... you never expect to live without. And then life reminds you daily that they are gone. You become disoriented and uncomfortable in these new realities, because your heart now carries permanent voids.

And all of it—every painful shift—was handed to me by something so inevitable: Transition.

THE INEVITABLE

"THERE IS A TIME FOR EVERYTHING, AND A SEASON FOR EVERY ACTIVITY UNDER THE HEAVENS..."

ECCLESIASTES 3:1 (KJV)

Transition is the process of shifting from one state to another. Sounds simple, right? But it's anything but. Transition is disruptive. Messy. Uncomfortable. And it rarely asks for your permission before it barges in.

Transition isn't just about a new location or changed circumstance — it's a divine summons to transform. To become new while releasing what was. But most of us cling to the familiar, even when it's dysfunctional. So we fight it. We resist forward movement because we're addicted to what used to be.

But here's the truth: Everything God made is transitional — not static, not fixed. The sun rises and sets because it has somewhere to go. Seasons shift because life demands growth. Even good things have an expiration date.

And still we resist. We cling to jobs that no longer fulfill us. Stay in relationships that expired long ago. Revisit places God already left. Why? Because transition exposes our lack of control. We don't choose the timing, the terms, or the terrain. We just get moved — and then spend the rest of the time trying to make sense of it.

And yet... this is the process. Not just a process, but the process.

I'll never forget one of my tantrums with God. I was on the floor — legs crossed, tears streaming — convinced nothing in my life was turning in my favor. Honestly, it felt like everything was getting worse. Mid-prayer I blurted, 'God, my circumstances aren't changing...' Before I could finish, He interrupted me: *'But you are.'*

And that was the revelation: transition wasn't about my circumstances shifting — it was about me shifting. God wouldn't change what was around me until He changed what was within me. That's what makes transition inevitable: not whether it comes, but what it creates.

Transition is not effective if the only thing that changes is your location. This is where many people miss it. They change jobs, cities, churches, even partners—but they never change themselves. Eventually, the old version of them shows up in the new place and sabotages everything God is trying to do.

Let me say it plainly: the goal of transition isn't to change it—the job, the zip code, the assignment. The goal of transition is to change you.

So here's the question you have to ask your heart: Am I changing in the direction of my next... or am I just going through the motions?

Because if your internal life doesn't shift, you'll carry bitterness into your blessings. You'll step into the new while secretly longing for the old. And that longing will blind you to the beauty of what's already in front of you.

YEA..WE CAN SEE THAT

Let's be extremely honest and clear—transition is traumatic. Not because you're in danger, but because you are inconveniently uncomfortable. You're suddenly placed in a space you didn't ask for, forced to navigate a new normal you weren't prepared for.

If transition had a sound, it wouldn't be the roar of bold confidence or the crescendo of a praise break. It would be the cry of a baby—loud, raw, and completely unfiltered. That's what transition feels like. It turns you into a child again. You cry often and can't fully explain why. You're not in danger, but you're unsettled. You're not unsafe, but you're shaken. You're being forced to come to grips with a reality you didn't choose—while somehow trying to preserve the dignity and wisdom of what the last season taught you. And honestly? It sucks.

The more you grow, the harder it becomes to keep living in what no longer fits. Growth demands release. But that's easier said than done. Because sometimes what you've outgrown is also what you've grown attached to. So you fight to hold on. You rationalize. You dress it up. You try to make it look presentable. But eventually, no matter how well you try to cover it, everyone around you can see how stuffed, strained, and stifled you really are.

You don't wear a winter coat in the summer. So why do we try to wear our old selves in new seasons?

Transition forces you to ask hard questions:
What am I still holding on to from what was?
What do I need to release so I can fully walk into what's next?
What part of me is God trying to free, but I keep clinging to out of fear or nostalgia?

Here's the reality—you're fighting to stay in what God is taking you away from. And that fight is exhausting. It's not just grief from what you've lost. It's the disorienting exhaustion of trying to learn how to live again. To find your footing again. To breathe in a space that doesn't yet feel like home.

Yes, you've been through transition before—but this one is different. This one doesn't feel safe. And let's be honest: the human heart craves safety. We crave familiarity. Even if it wasn't perfect, at least we knew how to function in the last place. This new space? It requires faith. And surrender. And waiting. It's frustrating because the path ahead is unclear, but the door behind you is already closed.

And if you're not careful, you'll try to carry everything from the last place with you—even the things you've outgrown.

If you know me, you know Junee is my heart. When he was around one or two years old, he had this white t-shirt that he absolutely loved. I mean loved. It didn't matter if it was clean or dirty—he wanted to wear it. All the time. At first, it was adorable. We laughed. Took pictures. Held on to the memory.

But then... Junee grew.

And the more he grew, the harder it became to get him out of that shirt. He'd cry. He'd fight us. He'd stretch it over his growing frame as if it still made sense. But no matter how much he loved it, the truth remained—the shirt didn't fit anymore.

Trying to live in what you've outgrown is not only uncomfortable—it eventually becomes obvious. You can try to make it work. You can dress it up. You can even pretend everything is fine. But deep down, everyone can see that it doesn't fit you anymore.

That's what happens when we resist transition. We keep trying to squeeze into relationships, roles, and identities that no longer serve us. And in His mercy, God keeps pulling us out of them. Even when it feels like He's stripping us.

That shirt was too small for Junee. Just like some seasons, assignments, and mindsets are too small for you now. And here's the hard truth: God is not trying to embarrass you—He's trying to evolve you.

So let it go.

Let go of what you've outgrown. Let go of what doesn't fit. Let go of the version of yourself that can't walk into what God has prepared.

Because staying in what no longer fits will only lead to frustration.

And trust me—you were made to grow.

"ARE YOU STUCK THOUGH?"

Let's be real—one of the hardest parts of transition is not knowing how long it's going to last. If God handed us a timeline, we could brace ourselves. We'd mark the calendar, count the days, and find ways to distract ourselves until it passed. But God doesn't operate that way. He gives you the promise, sometimes even a glimpse of the destination, but rarely does He provide an ETA.

And that's what breaks us—not the movement itself, but the waiting while moving. It's one thing to feel stuck when you haven't done anything. It's another to have obeyed God, taken the steps, left what was comfortable... and still feel like nothing is happening. That's the frustration of transition: you're not in control of the time, the terms, or the terrain. And for those of us who thrive on structure and certainty, that's terrifying.

In Matthew 14, the disciples are caught in a storm. The Bible says they were a "considerable distance from land." In other words, they were too far from where they started but still not close enough to where they were going. That's the middle. That space between obedience and arrival. The storm is raging, but what stands out is this: the boat never stops moving. It might have been slow. It might have been difficult. But it never said the boat was stuck. It never said it turned around. It never said the storm swallowed it. It just said the middle was hard.

This is what we miss when we idolize certainty and cling to schedules—we confuse delay with denial. We call the middle a mistake when really, it's the development zone. And the longer it takes, the more tempted we are to question everything. Did I hear God right? Is this still His will? Why isn't anything changing?

Here's the answer you may not want, but absolutely need: God is happening. He's not just getting you to a destination— He's making sure you're ready when you arrive. And that takes time.

It reminds me of flying. The pilot knows the destination, the turbulence forecast, and the arrival time—before the plane even leaves the ground. But we, the passengers, only know what the pilot chooses to tell us. Usually, it's the basics: "We'll be in the air for two hours." Or, "We're experiencing a delay." And most of the time, we're fine with that—because we trust the pilot.

But when it comes to God, suddenly we want the full flight manual. We want the route. The turbulence forecast. The reason for every bump. And when we don't get it, we spiral. We start checking the time. We assume we're lost. We imagine something is wrong—when really, we're still on course.

Turbulence doesn't mean you're off track. It just means you're in the air.
The boat can be in the will of God and still face a storm.
The plane can be perfectly aligned with the plan and still hit resistance.
So can you.

You're not off course.
You're not being punished.
You're in process.
And process takes time.

The issue isn't motion—it's trust. Can you keep riding without knowing when it ends? Can you stay seated without grabbing the wheel?

Because just like the pilot, God knows the speed, the direction, and the landing point. He knows how high to take you and when to bring you back down. The question is: Will you rest while He steers? Or will you keep throwing up panicked prayers like backseat directions, trying to control something that was never yours to manage?

This is surrender. Not just saying "Yes, Lord," but letting Him lead—even when it's silent, even when it's slow, even when it's stormy.

WHO PUT YOU IN CHARGE?

This is the part that stings. The real ugliness of transition isn't just the discomfort—it's the lack of control. You didn't sign up for this. You didn't initiate it. You didn't schedule the shift, select the timeline, or map out the detour. You were placed in it. Handed something you didn't ask for. Assigned to a process you didn't agree to. And because you didn't put yourself in it... you can't take yourself out.

That's what makes transition feel cruel at times. We're conditioned to believe that if we work hard enough, pray long enough, or stay positive enough, we can move things forward. But in seasons of transition, your effort doesn't give you the keys. You can't force the door open. You can't speed up the clock. You can't manipulate divine timing. This is where trust stops being a Christian buzzword and starts feeling like a burden. It's the moment you realize: I don't get to escape this just because I want to. You don't get to call timeout. You don't get to opt out. You have to endure it. And that doesn't always feel fair.

Especially when you know you didn't cause it.

You didn't ask for the layoff.
You didn't plan the loss.
You didn't anticipate the breakup, the diagnosis, the relocation, or the abrupt shift.

And now? You're stuck in the hallway between "what was" and "what's next." And no amount of crying, fasting, or forcing is unlocking the next season before its time. It's humbling. It's frustrating. And yes, it's ugly. This is the side of transition nobody really talks about. The part they don't preach about. The truth they don't tell you when you're on fire for God and shouting "Send me!"

Because here's the truth: God doesn't need your permission to move you.
He doesn't have to consult your calendar to interrupt your comfort.
When He says it's time—it's time.

You can either spend your energy fighting to return to what was, or you can surrender to the transformation happening in what is.

But one thing is certain—you're not going back.
And you don't get to skip ahead.

So what do you do? You sit in the middle. You pray in the middle. You cry in the middle. And if you're wise… you grow in the middle. Because trying to escape what God has intentionally placed you in is a wasted fight.

You didn't put yourself in it.
So you can't take yourself out.

"CAN I CATCH A BREAK OR IS THAT AGAINST POLICY NOW? IT'S GIVING: ONE STORM ENDS, ANOTHER CLOCKS IN FOR THE NEXT SHIFT. I MUST HAVE THE 'JOSH CAN HANDLE IT, GO CRAZY' TRIAL PACKAGE

HEY GOD,
IS YOU COO ?!!

Do we have beef?
Like..is there something I'm missing?
Is my life like this because I've done something wrong?
I don't get it.
It's just one thing after another.
And God... You know I love You.
You know my heart.
I'm flawed, yeah—but for real, if there's something I need to fix, just show me. I'll fix it. I'll let it go. Whatever it is. Just show me.
Because this sucks. It doesn't seem fair.
It feels like the people who don't even acknowledge You are out here living carefree, winning—and here I am trying to live what You showed me... trying to be real, trying to impact people the right way... and life just keeps falling apart.
So I gotta ask:
Did I miss You? Did I miss the mark?
Am I out of alignment?
Are You even pleased with me?

I'm struggling with that question.
I read, "When a man's ways please the Lord, even his enemies will be at peace with him."
But I'm not seeing peace. I'm not feeling it.
So I look inward—am I the problem?
I'm trying to be a good sport through this.
Trying to navigate this season "the right way."
But what even is the right way?
I retreat... that feels wrong.
I try to stay quiet so I don't mislabel the season... that feels wrong too.
I feel the weight of depression and I don't know what to make of it.
I feel like I'm at my breaking point.
And I just want to know
Is this my fault?
Is there anything I can do to make this better? Different?
God, I just don't know.
And You know how much that bothers me.
I'm trying to turn my brain off...
But I don't know how.

2.
HOW DID YOU GET HERE?

I love music. If you've not discovered by now, I'm a huge entertainment buff—film, television, and music. I'm a 90s baby, and I believe I grew up in one of the greatest eras of music to date. One of my favorite pastimes in grade school was going to what we called in Oak Cliff a Sock Hop. Sock Hops were simply school dances, and I never understood the name—but the assignment was always understood.

Because we were in the "hood," we always added extra flair to our songs. I don't know how anybody else listened to music, but we talked back to our favorite songs. I remember being in the car listening to Sir Charles Jones' song Friday and yelling out, "WHO THIS FOR, SIR?" before his opening lyric—"This one is dedicated, for all my workers who work 9 to 5." The song just gets better when you talk to it.

One of my favorite songs to date is still Deborah Cox's Nobody's Supposed to Be Here. Picture it—you're at the Sock Hop, you hear the beat drop, and you know what time it is. Considering what I just told you—we talk back to the song. As the music builds, so does the extreme theatrics leading up to the introductory question. In concert, everyone sings from their diaphragm, "How did you get here?" Once asked, in response to the question, everyone shouts my favorite part... "MANN I CAUGHT THE BUS." Even typing this out put the biggest smile on my face.

I've always loved that experience of call and response to song... it isn't a good song unless it makes you talk back to it. As jovial as we are in singing that addition, what it reveals to me is the innate human curiosity to always solve for how and why.

"Why" is my most favorite question to ask. It's the first question I ask in my consults before starting a new project or saying yes. I'm extremely analytical, be it good or bad. So whenever I run into trouble in life, my first stop is with myself like, "Ok, Josh, what could you have done wrong?"

Many of us think like this, and it's highly problematic—but it's not your fault. We've been conditioned by church, by dogmatic communicators of the "gospel," and church folk alike to assume unfavorable things are happening to us because we've offended God in some kind of way.

This isn't a new revelation. When you read your Bible and witness stories like Job's, you see that he is described as a blameless man. Yet when turmoil hits his life, his friends who supposedly "know God" pinpoint the reason for him going through all he faced as being God's punishment for Job offending Him.

If we take a look in the New Testament, we meet a blind man who is surrounded by people asking Jesus, "Why is this man blind? Who sinned—his mother or his father?" To which Jesus responds, "Neither."

Sometimes obedience feels like somebody took your journal, put it to music, and hit repeat on the parts you'd rather skip. It's the soundtrack of surrender — and it doesn't always sound pretty.

At large, my issue—or rather, disdain—with the "church" and its folks is that they don't really know the nature, character, nor the method of the God that they so dogmatically "defend" and "speak for." This plagues me, because to the unlearned it creates this false narrative that people take as truth: that trouble means you've missed God, and that peace means you're in His will.

This kind of narrative makes God seem petty—and He's not. He's not sitting on the throne monitoring bad behavior and giving tally marks of trouble to people who misstep. That's the perpetual lie that many of us have been fed for years, and it forces us to "obey" because we don't want to get in trouble with God. Because of this, you assume that when storms hit your life it is God's punishment. Sorry, I don't mean to come off insensitive—but that's quite laughable.

No, you didn't get here because you caught the bus like we playfully called back to Deborah Cox. May I suggest to you: you are here—in a storm, in unfavorable circumstances, etc.—not because you're separated from Him, but because you messed around and got close.

I know, you're saying to yourself, "Well, that can't be it. I thought getting closer to God meant that my life would know more peace. I'd laugh more than I cried, smile more than I frown." But the reality is—and let me hold your hand when I say this—your proximity to God is why and how you got here. Your obedience is why you're experiencing "hell," not your rebellion.

People idolize getting close to God for the aesthetic they think it gives to other people, but the reality is being close isn't glamorous at all—it's quite literally ghetto. YES, I said that.

Now, before you pick up religious rocks of heresy, let me give you basis for that claim. This book, again, is built upon the back of Matthew 14. In this text, we find the story of Jesus feeding the five thousand with two fish and five loaves of bread—this is a miracle. Pay attention to the text, though. The disciples have proximity to Jesus and they make Him aware of the hunger of the crowd, to which Jesus tells them in so many words, "You see the need—you fix it."

The problem is the need outweighs the resource. This is a very large crowd; the five thousand does not include women or children. Now the disciples bring to Jesus' attention that the crowd needs to go home because they've been there all day and haven't eaten. If the crowd hasn't eaten, then we can logically deduce that the disciples haven't either.

Here's why I say being close sucks: Jesus multiplies the limited resources they had, but doesn't give it to them to enjoy. He gives it to them to distribute. The disciples have been there all day too, but they don't get the luxury to sit and eat. In their own hunger, they have to pass out what's not meant for them to consume—yet. Imagine fixing plates for others while your stomach bites your liver. They contribute to a miracle they aren't the recipient of, although they need it too.

This isn't just one instance. You see repeatedly in scripture that the crowds get the miracle while the close facilitate them. The close sometimes seem ignored.

Another witness I would like to bring to the stand is Lazarus. In John 11, scripture makes it known that Jesus has relationship with not just Lazarus but also with Mary and Martha. They are His friends, which means He knows them and they know Him.

I won't bore you with the story—we know it. Lazarus gets deathly ill. His sisters send word to Jesus. He receives the word in time to make it on time, but intentionally chooses not to rush to his friend's deathbed. He chooses to stay where He was two extra days. They don't have cars, there is no jet; they are traveling by foot. Staying two extra days automatically sets them back. Remember, though, Lazarus is deathly ill, and their message is one of urgency—but Jesus chooses to chill and relax. He doesn't even reply back to them. He leaves them on read.

Now Jesus is grown. He can rock out and do whatever He decides to do—but I have an issue with this because the text exposes that this is His dear friend. When people who are close call me, I drop everything and go—because that's what being dependable and a friend is about. But I'm not Jesus.

But my biblical beef with Jesus is born, because I read a story about a blind man by the name of Bartimaeus, whom Jesus does not know, getting a miracle immediately. If that's not enough, there is a man named Jairus, also whom Jesus does not know or have relationship with, who has a sick daughter that's about to die—and Jesus doesn't hesitate to go to his house. In fact, on His way to Jairus' house, He's interrupted by a woman who doesn't even have a name—just a label: the woman who had been bleeding for twelve years—who also receives an immediate miracle.

Finally, this is the one that really pushed me over the edge. There is a centurion man who seeks out Jesus because he has a daughter dying at home. Once Jesus hears this guy's story, He initiates the house visit and says, "Okay, let's get to her." The centurion ruler says, "Oh no, I don't need you to go to my house, it's too messy—just speak the word only and it will be done." Jesus is impressed by this man's faith and speaks and boom—daughter is IMMEDIATELY healed.

This blew me, because it proved that Jesus didn't even have to physically be there to make a miracle happen. So help me understand—how are all of these strangers getting immediate miracles, but the one you are close with, that you love, that you have relationship with—you take your time? They couldn't even get a reply, a "Hey, I'm not going to make it in time." That's not ghetto to you all?

When you are close, you don't get the miracles—you become them. You become what and who God uses to birth belief in those that don't know Him. While that is seemingly glorious, we have to tell the truth about how agonizing that is as well.

Imagine the talk back afterwards and Lazarus coming to the realization that, "I became sick and died, not because You were mad at me, but because You trusted my life to bring You glory." — Read that line again.

And here's the part I need you to sit with—you're not here because you missed Him. You're here because you messed around and got close.

That's why it hurts. That's why it feels unfair. That's why you feel overlooked. Because closeness doesn't always look like favor... sometimes it comes with responsibility.

"IMMEDIATELY JESUS MADE THE DISCIPLES GET INTO THE BOAT AND GO ON AHEAD OF HIM TO THE OTHER SIDE..."

MATTHEW 14:22 (NIV)

Obedience sounds beautiful until it costs you. Folks make it seem like saying yes to God means blessing on blessing — but sometimes it feels like the opposite: like your yes signed you up for struggle instead of reward.

I want to say this very plainly to you: your yes is the reason for the storm you're facing. This is not an attempt to detour you from saying yes—but a chin check for your temper tantrum.

There are terms and conditions that precede your yes. In those terms and conditions, there is a clause of sovereignty. This clause says that you relinquish your right to comfort, control, and convenience while yielding to God's complete will, way, and time. This clause reveals that your yes is not to victory laps and flower fields of ease—but rather to commitment to enduring involuntary suffering.

Involuntary suffering is the pain you didn't choose but couldn't avoid—because God chose you. It's the pain you didn't earn, the trial you didn't initiate, the storm you didn't stir up. It's not because you're rebellious—it's because you're responsive. And that's what makes it hard to wrap your mind around. Because we're taught that pain is punishment. That hardship means you must have messed up. But there's another kind of pain—the kind that comes after you obey.

HANDPICKED

You didn't choose the storm, but you chose Him. And He chose to use the storm as part of your becoming.

I can hear you now, wrestling with the reality that your obedience does not guarantee a painless, trouble-less, or easygoing life. We don't like that kind of theology. We'd rather believe that obedience makes everything easier. That saying "yes" to God means walking into blessing after blessing. But sometimes, your "yes" puts you on a collision course with the very storm you were hoping to avoid.

And maybe that's why Peter's story hits so hard. Because obedience didn't land him in calm waters — it placed him right in the storm..

The Bible says that Jesus made the disciples get into the boat and go ahead of Him to the other side. He didn't suggest it. He didn't ask for volunteers. He made them go. And it was after obeying Him—after getting in the boat, after launching out—that they found themselves in the middle of a storm.

I thought obedience meant peace — but it introduced me to problems. I thought it meant clarity — but it gave me more questions. I thought it meant joy — but it left me wrestling with frustration. Obedience wasn't a shortcut to ease — it was an invitation to trust.

That messes with our logic.

This is the side of obedience we don't talk about enough. We glamorize the call but rarely tell the truth about the cost. Sometimes, God will lead you straight into the middle of a storm—not to harm you, but to develop something in you that couldn't be formed any other way.

And the first lie you'll have to silence is the one that says, "If you were really doing what God said, this wouldn't be happening." I'll never forget a revelation God gave me in the middle of a tantrum—keep your judgment, yes I have them frequently.

The revelation was this: "It's not chaos, it's alignment."

Alignment sometimes mirrors what we deem adversity.

So let me put your mind at ease—you're not here because of what you did wrong. You're here because of what you got right.

I would call Job to the stand to testify, but I don't want to beat a dead horse. I'll move my plow.

TRUTH IS

My mom ran a tight ship (household) when I was coming up. Our house was very restrictive. Simply put, if it had no ties to the church, nine times out of ten, we couldn't do it. This meant no girls—unless my mom knew there was absolutely no attraction (which I learned how to play to my benefit, but I digress). If it wasn't gospel music, oh, it was not played in our house.

I remember singing what she called "worldly music" and immediately being chastised. "This is a saved house, and everything in here is going to be saved. If you don't want to be saved, as long as you're in here, you're gonna act like you saved."

Long story short, if you weren't family, a church member, or someone she approved—you weren't coming over. And even then, some of them were limited.

My mom loved her house CLEAN. Spick and span. If the entire house was clean but there was a dirty plate and fork in the sink, it was, "I thought I told y'all to clean up my house. I want it spotless."

Saturday mornings were not cartoon and cereal days or days to lounge around. Early Saturday mornings, my sister and I were met with the loudness of John P. Kee's *Strength* album blaring from the speakers and her shouting, "Get on up! Today is clean-up day." Clean-up day was not just taking trash out—no, we were breaking down beds, washing floorboards and window sills.

I'm as clean as I am today because of this.

Growing up, I had a favorite cousin. His name is Jacob. We were thick as thieves. I loved being around him, he loved being around me, and when we were together a good time was guaranteed. We would take turns going to each other's houses, because what teenage boy doesn't like a break from his mom?

In my opinion, his mom was way nicer than mine—at least to me. He could ask his mom if I could come over, and her answer was always yes. My mom adored a "No," so while he boldly asked his mom, I tiptoed to ask mine.

Because I knew cleanliness was pleasing to my mom, I learned how to do what she wanted so I could get what I wanted. This is where the overachiever in me was born. I knew if I only did what was required of me, that wouldn't yield the fruit I wanted.

Cleaning my room would've been met with, "That's what you're supposed to do." I soon discovered that by cleaning my room, her room, and the entire house, I could get her to lean heavily to the "yes" side of the spectrum. It went from "That's what you're supposed to do," to "Josh, what do you want?"

I had the master key.

I shared that story in hopes to parallel our "obedience" to God. We don't obey because we love Him—we obey because we've convinced ourselves that our obedience is the equivalent of a dog getting its favorite treat for doing what we want it to do.

So we fast and pray heavily when we want sickness out of our bodies. We're faithful in giving when we want God to bless us with a new job with more money. We're kinder to each other when we want God to bless us.

We believe if we feed God our good behavior, then He is obligated to do what we want Him to do—and when He doesn't, we feel played and start withholding ourselves and our obedience as a form of punishment to Him.

Let's call Lazarus' sister Mary to the stand.

In John 11, the scripture distinguishes this Mary from the other Marys in the Bible. It says, "This is the Mary that poured expensive perfume on Jesus and wiped His feet with her hair." Now when we meet Mary and Martha, Mary is at Jesus' feet learning while Martha is busy making sure the house is clean for Him.

This time around, though, the roles are reversed. Martha is the first one in Jesus' presence, and Mary is missing. My question in reading the text is: why is Mary missing now?

Here is what we can logically deduce from the text—Mary's posture and position changed when she didn't get the result she thought her worship warranted. The one who was at His feet before her brother died is now missing now that he's dead.

Like many of us, Mary retaliates to God's sovereignty by withholding her presence from Him when she doesn't get what she wants from Him. This reveals a heart posture that needs to be confronted—which is the one that says, "I'm only here for what You can do and give me. I'll celebrate Your hand but dishonor Your sovereignty."

Let me gently suggest to you that this isn't obedience at all—it's nothing more than masked coercion and manipulation. I know that one was tough, so I'll hold your hand for this one:

Obedience does not result in your desired outcome.

Real obedience doesn't even concern itself with the outcome. True obedience says, "God, I've done what You've asked of me, and that's my pleasure."

What we discover now is that many of us are not obedient—we are conditionally compliant. We'll do what God requires... as long as it benefits us.

WHAT'S IN IT FOR ME?

This is where I echo the words of Jesus—"I tell you a hard thing." God has not called you to be performative, but to be postured.

This breeds the question I feel in your heart of hearts: "Well, what's the point? What's the point of being obedient if there's no benefit?"

This heart posture is the reason many live a life of unspoken and unresolved resentment toward God—because you thought obedience brought you what you want.

The truth of obedience is simply this: you don't obey for, you obey from. From reverence. From love. From trust.

While there are biblical benefits for being obedient, they are not the reason for you to be obedient. When you obey for — what, you tell God, "I want it more than I want You."

Deuteronomy 28, in the wrong hands, is nothing more than a setup for one to be at odds with God. If it is not studied correctly, you'll walk around performative and entitled, thinking that God owes you something materialistic as a reward for your obedience. And the opposite would be that you walk around defeated and in fear when you disobey, as if God is going to give you the Job experience and take everything from you.

Being blessed in the city and in the field, blessed going out and coming in, the head and not the tail, above and not beneath, the lender and not the borrower—is not the promise of a soft life. Those blessings are not invincibility, money out the wazoo, and a life of no pain or trial.

It is God's protection clause.

I'm not invincible—I'm protected. And protection is the real bag. Protection says you'll be thrown in the fire but you won't be burned. You'll be tossed in the lion's den, but instead of you being their meal, I'll make them your pillow. The water that you're supposed to drown in—I'll make solid ground for you.

It is God rebuking the devourer. Obedience is your covering. A life of disobedience is a life uncovered and unprotected. The lion may be a pillow to you—until it gets hungry. Who knows?

There is nothing wrong with desiring a soft life. But soberly, I want to tell you—

Your obedience does not result in a soft life.

May the lie that suggests you've missed Him because it's hard be broken off of your life.

May your obedience stem from a postured heart and not for perks.

May the disappointment and resentment you have toward God bring you to repentance and resolve.

May the purpose of God rise higher than the pain you feel.

And finally, may your storm forever be proof that you are close — not that He's angry.

So if you're asking yourself, 'How did I get here?' — remember this: obedience brought you. And if obedience brought you, obedience will keep you. The same hand that called you out won't let you sink.

"I'M TIRED OF THE UP & DOWN... THE BACK AND FORTH.. TAKE ME OUT THE CHAT....NOW"

HEY GOD,

NOTHING FEELS STABLE

I'm overwhelmed— because I have so much in me and on me that I just need to get out.

I don't like that everything feels unstable right now— relationships, work, money, even church. I'm being stretched and pulled in so many directions that me— the actual person—is feeling neglected.

If I'm honest, I feel like I'm only a product or a service. Like as long as I show up and do my job, that's all that matters. But my feelings matter too. I want to be considered. I want people to move heaven and earth for me, the same way I've done for them. I want to be treated with the same level of goodness I freely extend. My wanting to disappear isn't me giving up—it's a tactic of self-preservation.

I'm tired of having to save myself.

I'm tired of having to restore myself.

I sit in solitude because I treat me well, and I just want to be in spaces that treat me well too. I still long for reciprocity.

I don't want to feel like I'm begging for it—or like I have to work to prove my worthiness. I want what's genuine. I want mutuality. I want to be poured into too—not just constantly pouring out.

This is not the job for me. I don't see myself here long-term. This is sucking the life out of me. The systems, the structure, the lack of help and support... it feels like, yet again, I'm only kept around for what I can produce. I don't thrive in those spaces.

I want my fulfillment to matter—not just to me, but to my employer.

I want to be placed in environments where I can thrive and where I know I will thrive.

It's like trying to plant a tree that needs sunlight, water, and rich soil in a place where those things are scarce—and still telling it to grow.

I long for stability and security—because those things bring me peace.

dear God... I just want peace.

3.
SAFE·ISH

Picture it—September 2023. I'm a month into living in a very spacious five-bedroom home with a super open kitchen that's perfect for my kickbacks and game nights. There's a pool and hot tub in the backyard with a fully furnished patio in between them. This was my first taste of homeownership, and it tasted like a perfectly fried pork chop with collard greens, macaroni and cheese, and sweet cornbread to accompany it—this is my favorite meal, in case you ever want to feed me.

I wake up to what is seemingly a normal day, besides the fact that I woke up early—which I never do. I'm a few hours shy of the time I'm supposed to be at work, so I decide to do something productive with the extra time. I get myself together, grab the leashes for the dogs, and we head out the door for a morning walk.

The walk is serene, and I begin to pray and thank God for a new day and all the things I'm grateful for. Now, when I get in the vein of prayer, I get lost in it—like my uncle during grace on Thanksgiving. By this time, I'm a few miles in, going from a slow walk to almost a jog. I look at the dogs, and they're looking at me like, Alright, this was fun, but now it's time to go in the house.

I pick up on their social cues and put a pretty bowtie on my prayer:

> "You know what, Father? I'm tired of not fully trusting You. You are good, and I know You don't have any ill will toward me, so this morning I fully surrender. I relinquish my right to control my life.

You are God; You can do anything and everything, and nothing can stop Your plan. In Jesus' name— Amen."

I exhale deeply and head back to the house. I still have some time before work, so I sing my favorite songs in the shower, iron my clothes, and head out the door. I'm feeling good—me and Jesus have talked, I did a great thing in surrendering, and I'm even early for work. This is a great day.

I make it to my desk, sign into my systems, laugh and joke with a few of my coworkers—a typical day. I'm working, replying to emails, and looking at my tasks for the day when my office phone rings. Our HR director is on the other side of the line, very sweetly asking for my presence in the conference room for a quick meeting. I think nothing of it; I'm always called into a meeting.

I walk into the conference room and see the HR director, the accounting director, and the VP of my department already seated. I take my seat, but no one is making eye contact with me. She greets me and then jumps right in:

> "Hey Josh, so we called you into this meeting this morning very briefly just to let you know that we've decided that today is your last day. We'll pay you up to today, and you'll get any vacation and PTO you've not used paid out to you, but yes—as of this moment, you're no longer an employee here. I'll retrieve your key card and will walk you over to your office to collect your things."

The air in the room feels heavier now. I could hear the hum of the ceiling vent over her voice. I swear the air got colder, though no one touched the thermostat.

Considering the prayer I prayed that morning, I replied, "Okay," chuckled at God's sense of humor, collected my things, and went back home. I wasn't distraught—at least, not in the moment. Maybe it was adrenaline, but I was okay. They mentioned they weren't going to fight my unemployment and there were no offenses listed as to why this decision was made, so I just accepted what God allowed and went on my way.

That peace of mind lasted until I discovered how unemployment worked and realized they were giving me something to put toward my bills—not necessarily enough to cover them. There was still a huge deficit. I love stability and security, and now both were threatened.

Just a week ago, mornings smelled like coffee and possibility. Now, they smelled like my own breath under the covers, because I didn't want to get up.

Because I am the over-thinker that I am, I immediately tried to put together pay periods with bill periods—and no matter how many periods I put together, I kept coming up with question marks. My peace swiftly became paralyzing stress that began rocking my world month after month. I stopped laughing as much and started panicking way more. Easily irritable, darkness became my friend, my bed my jail cell, and I was fully depressed. How could a great morning prayer walk result in this vicissitude?

Life became hard to bear—just moved into this house, now feeling like a failure, concerned with how things would look, where I would go, how things would turn out. I became the personification of anxiety. I'm not a fan of disruptions, and this quickly turned into resentment, shame, and low self-worth. I felt like I was failing at life and that I was—yet again—at the top of God's "strongest soldiers" list.

I threw many tantrums during this time because life was hitting from all angles all at once. My stability was in question, and nothing felt safe or stable.

One morning, I woke up with a heavy impression that God wanted to speak to me. That makes some people shout because they get cute, Instagram-post-worthy words to carry them through the week. But when God speaks to me? He's always slapping me across the back of my neck with His sandal—and that's exactly what He did.

I braced myself. God's voice never tiptoes into my life—He comes kicking doors open.

"*I never promised you that life would be stable. I promised that I would be stable — never leaving you.*

I never promised you that the boat would make it... I promised that you would.

If your metric for where I am is stability, you'll miss Me... because I was in the eye of the storm.

I will be your peace in the middle of it, but peace is not always the reward for obedience. Peace is a resolve, not a circumstance.

Your peace should rest on My presence with you, not on the absence or the calming of the storm.

My goal is not to make your life stable. My goal is to make you stable.

Stability that leads to a soft life was never My promise. That's the hope of your heart—not the covenant of Mine."
~ God

I had become someone I didn't know or enjoy but still had the weight of so much responsibility on my back. I'm not one to ask for help, because in the times I did before, it was either a no or it was thrown in my face later. I was meeting people who thought I was great, but I couldn't fully show up because deep down I was hoping we never had to go somewhere that cost money. I was serving heavily in church—being a light to others while my own light was going dim. I was drowning and didn't know what to do, but I knew something needed to be done.

After a ton of Google searches on how to turn your brain off, not let anxiety ruin and run your life, and how to combat depression—I ended up back where it started. I started walking again. Google told me that regular exercise, walking, jogging, and all the things alike would trick your brain into not stressing and worrying. That was a lie. But I continued to walk because it gave me something to do.

One of those walks, though, changed my life forever.

Growing up in a performance-based culture, you're celebrated for what you can do. For years—most of my life even—I was a doer. I noticed, though, how unkind I was to myself because I couldn't do anymore. I couldn't find words of encouragement to give to myself, and I didn't want to talk to other people because their responses were cliché and really got on my nerves. So I turned to affirmation albums on Apple Music.

As I walked, I would let them play, and the ones I liked I would repeat aloud. I'll never forget this moment because I literally stopped in the middle of the street, flabbergasted at the affirmation I had just heard. It was so simple yet so powerful.

RELAX A LITTLE

Safety is an innate human desire that is woven into both our biology and psychology. Safety is a fundamental need of humans—both physically and emotionally. We want love that is safe, family that is safe; everything pertaining to us, we want it to feed our sense of safety. What we don't talk enough about, though, is how we've made safety synonymous with comfort. And the moment life gets uncomfortable, we assume something must be wrong. 'This must not be God," we say, as if the Holy Spirit only moves in ergonomic chairs and quiet coffee shops. As I crossed the street, that affirmation gave my heart so much resolve because it gave me language. Here I was—living a life of fear and feeling endangered—all because life was not as convenient as it once was. This fear gripped my life and immobilized me.

Naturally, I'm wired not to let anything overtake me. I've always believed fear is just a lack of information, so I began to study different things in hopes of bringing mobility back into my life. What I came to know was both liberating and confrontational.

Did you know that humans are only born with two innate fears? Only two. Think about all the things you fear—from Freddy Krueger to snakes and spiders. You're only afraid of those things because you have been conditioned to be. Studies show that we are only born with the fear of falling and the fear of loud noises. Every other fear you have— you've acquired.

I'll be honest—immediately after reading that, I worked overtime trying to disprove it. My claustrophobia? Traced to something I saw happen to someone else. My trypophobia? Stems from trauma I saw happen with or to someone else. It's never been my experience, but I built a fear out of the hope that it would never become my experience—and that has brought so much limitation to my life. I'd embraced and defended fears I picked up along the way like they came with me in my original packaging.

Fear is nothing more than an illusion—no matter how hard you try to defend yours.

So let's discuss this fear of falling we're born with, because it's way deeper than breaking a limb.

> **falling** (adjective) — moving from a higher to a lower level, typically rapidly and without control.

Based on that definition alone, we can deduce that falling is only scary because we have no control once it happens. So then I would argue that the issue with falling is not the fall itself, but the how, where, why, and when.

Controlled, graceful falls? We're okay with those. Declines we can assess and measure? We make accommodations for those. But take away our right to facilitate it, and that's where the problem lies.

We love control, and anything we can't control we deem a threat to our safety. We spend years, lifetimes, and insurmountable resources trying to prevent falls—not because we don't want to fall, but because our fear of falling points us to an even bigger issue: our pride.

> **pride** (noun) — consciousness of one's own dignity.

YOU'RE LYING TO YOURSELF

Let me be honest with you—I'm what you'd call a performative extrovert. You'd think I'm the life of the party—and sometimes I am—but only when I feel safe. You get my best when I'm surrounded by familiar faces and spaces. But in new spaces? I retreat to the corner, analyzing every movement like I'm trying to crack the code of human interaction. Happens every time.

Here's the twist though: I'm also an entertainer. Put me on stage and give me a mic, and I'll light the room up. But take away the character, the script, the performance, and leave me with just me? I shrink. Why? Because performing gives me control. Vulnerability doesn't. And control feels safe… until it isn't.

I remember hating the barbershop. Not just because of the long waits, missed appointment times, bad breath, or the inappropriate conversations—but because it was one of the first places I felt exposed. Less-than. Not "boy enough."

I've always felt safer with women. My formative years weren't the prettiest—very traumatic—and much of that trauma came at the hands of males. I didn't play sports; I liked to act and be funny. I was rejected a lot, and being around boys was always about how many numbers you could get—that wasn't my speed. I was shy.

So the barbershop became the intensification of all I was not. I loved getting short cuts because the shorter they cut my hair, the less often I'd have to go.

There was a shop I preferred that was attached to the salon where my mom got her hair done. Smaller, more familiar. They knew my name, knew what I was into, and the women would flirt with me and call me handsome—I especially liked that part.

But eventually, I got sent to the bigger barbershop closer to the house. Multiple barbers, loud banter, and a thick cloud of masculinity that made me want to disappear. To make matters worse, my mom wouldn't even stay—she'd drop me off and leave to run errands. I was alone. My palms are sweating now just reliving it. Surrounded by everything that made me uncomfortable—men, their judgment, their unspoken expectations.

This was real for me. I hated it. And I made a vow to myself that I would not have to be subjected to that kind of environment again. So, when college came, I avoided the whole thing. I taught myself to cut my own hair, and I haven't been back to a barbershop since 2011.

Control was safer than exposure.

It's important that we not only investigate the visible behaviors we seek to prevent, but also the why behind them. Behind every action, there is a root—I know this because I'm extremely introspective.

Regardless of how big or small, beneficial or detrimental the behavior is, there is always a deeper reason for it. I hide my boxes of Little Debbie cakes—not because I don't like to share, but because I like to share on my terms. Growing up, my family would eat whatever was in the house—whether it was theirs or not.

I thought I was protecting myself, but really, I was isolating myself. That's what self-preservation does. It takes your comfort, safety, and security into your own hands because you don't feel anyone else will. It disguises itself as strength, but it's really pride in survival clothes.

And pride—it comes before the fall. Not always the loud kind of fall. Sometimes, it's the quiet kind. The fall from trust. The fall from intimacy. The fall from surrender.

Our pride in controlling how people see us keeps us from fully trusting God's protection. We secretly believe He might abandon us too—like they did. And can I humbly submit to you that the real threat to your safety is your pride? It's believing you have enough strength, tools, and fortitude to keep yourself better than God can.

" NOW UNTO HIM THAT IS ABLE TO KEEP YOU FROM FALLING..."

JUDE 1:24 (KJV)

Coming up in church, I heard this doxology at the end of every service. It did something to my spirit—even without my full understanding of it. This verse emphasizes God's active involvement in divinely protecting us and ensuring stability.

Let's slow down. Put an imaginary line between "Him" and "that."

"Now unto Him..." — Most of our frustration comes from trying to assume roles that don't belong to us. The text does not say "Now unto me" or "Now unto us." This isn't a joint effort—it's not a collaboration. We don't have the wherewithal to keep ourselves.

My nickname for God is Mastermind. He's so careful and calculated that it's impossible for you to slip through the cracks. You don't know enough to be able to keep you. God is an overhead orchestrator, not a lateral one—you know what you see; He knows what it is.

Here's a hard truth: God is never going to give you so much of anything that it makes you His equal. If you could keep yourself from falling, wouldn't you have successfully done it by now?

Let's take into account the next phrase: *"that is able to keep you from falling..."* — here's where I want to plant my plow for a bit. If you're anything like me, you immediately question what falling actually means. Because I've messed up plenty of times since I've been saved—you have too, it's okay to tell the truth.

So what does it truly mean to fall?

I don't like to make anything up, so I went back to the beginning—the garden—where the fall of man took place. Here's what I discovered:

Sin, by definition, means to miss the mark. I'm an actor, and in both stage and film we have what's called marks—specific positions where the actor should stand or move for proper camera framing, shot focus, and overall continuity.

To miss your mark means you're standing somewhere you weren't supposed to be. The mark is taped on the ground, and when you miss it, you jeopardize the flow of the entire scene.

The same principle works spiritually. Missing the mark means you're somewhere God didn't design for you to be—but it's not the end of the world. A missed mark is simply an opportunity for the Director to redirect and reposition you.

Now here's where it gets deeper: in Genesis 3, we see both sin and the fall. They're not the same thing.

The sin was that Adam was with her—silent—and participated in her misstep.

The fall was Adam believing another voice over God's.

Sin is the act. The fall is the shift in belief.
Sin is missing the mark. The fall is abandoning the truth for a lie.

This is why falling is so dangerous—it's not just tripping over a temptation; it's trusting the wrong voice to lead you afterward.

So how does God keep us from falling?

He keeps us with something called—the thorn.

Paul talks about his thorn in 2 Corinthians 12:7–9, and we tend to focus on how it feels—painful, limiting, humiliating. But the real question is: What was it for?

Paul says it was given to him. And gifts, according to James 1:17, come from God. That means this wasn't punishment—it was intentional protection.

The first thorn shows up in Genesis 3 after Adam's fall—symbolizing sin, sorrow, and hardship. Adam got thorns as punishment. But in Matthew 27, Jesus—the second Adam—takes those thorns, and they're twisted into a crown.

Now here's where the revelation deepens:
A crown is a symbol of victory, authority, and position. It's placed on the head—the seat of thought and belief. The soldiers thought they were mocking Jesus by making His crown out of thorns, but in Kingdom logic, they were doing something ceremonial. They were declaring that Jesus had conquered sin, sorrow, and hardship—the very things thorns represented since Genesis.

And they didn't just place the crown gently; they beat it into His head. Why? Because the enemy's primary target has always been the mind. Adam's fall in the garden wasn't simply eating the fruit—it was a shift in belief. He fell because he believed another voice over God's. That's why Jesus had to redeem not just our souls, but our thinking.

The crown of thorns says to every believer:

Your sin has been paid for.

Your sorrows have been carried.

Your hardships have been conquered.

It's not just a crown of suffering—it's a crown of securing. It says, I've taken what was meant to harm you and turned it into a declaration that you already have the victory.

And here's the part that makes me shout: Scripture records that the soldiers took back their robe and their staff, but there is no verse that says they ever took the crown off His head. That crown went with Him all the way to Calvary. The stripes on His back healed our bodies. The blood He shed saved our souls. But the crown on His head redeemed our minds.

They beat that crown into His head so that sin, sorrow, and hardship wouldn't have to be beaten into yours.

So when God gave Paul a thorn, He wasn't handing him a random affliction—He was giving him a piece of that crown. The thorn didn't come from the ground; it came from the victory Jesus already wore.

It was there to keep Paul from falling—because the same pride that got Satan kicked out of heaven is the same pride that can sneak into a gifted, called, and anointed life.

The thorn is God's way of saying, I love you too much to let you trip over the same pride that caused the first fall. I'll keep you close, even if I have to keep you humble.

Paul says the thorn is "a messenger of Satan." Satan's message has always been accusation—You're not enough. You're disqualified. You can't be trusted. You don't belong.

He didn't give Paul the thorn (just like in Genesis, he didn't create the tree)—but he twists the truth about it. Satan will hold your thorn in front of you as proof that you're unworthy. God holds it as proof that you're protected.

Even a rose has thorns—not to disqualify its beauty, but to guard it. The thorn on a rose isn't there to make it less—it's there to keep it from being easily taken or destroyed.

Your thorn is the same. It's not there to ruin your life—it's there to keep you alive in your calling. This is why God told Paul "no" three times about removing it. You're only focused on how the thorn feels. God says, I know what the thorn is for.

It's there—as prescribed in the Scripture—to keep you from being conceited. God's "no" is not an injustice but rather an act of love. It says, I love you too much to let history repeat itself. I'm not going to remove My protection from you.

I know you cry over your thorn, but I've learned to shout over mine.

WHAT'S IT GONNA BE?

Fear never really leaves — it just changes clothes. One day it wears doubt, the next hesitation, and sometimes it dresses up as shame.

When we talk about the fear of falling, we can't ignore how our bodies and minds instinctively react to perceived danger. Fear isn't always a spiritual attack—it's also a built-in human survival system designed by God to alert us when something feels unsafe.

That's where Fight, Flight, and Freeze come in. These are the automatic responses our brains trigger when we feel threatened—whether the threat is physical, emotional, or spiritual.

In the context of this chapter, these responses matter deeply because fear of falling—whether into failure, embarrassment, or unbelief—can push us into one of three modes: fight, flight, or freeze. And understanding these responses doesn't just explain why we react the way we do, it helps us recognize the subtle ways we might be protecting ourselves in ways that actually keep us from the safety God provides.

For some of us, the instinct is to fight. We overcompensate to prove we're in control. In life, it looks like over-performing, micromanaging, or pushing people away before they get close enough to hurt you. Spiritually, it looks like defending yourself instead of letting God defend you.

The trap? Pride dressed up as strength. But the truth is this: the thorn is already proof that you're protected. You don't have to fight to prove it.

Others of us respond with flight. We escape before anyone notices we might fall. In life, it looks like ducking out of rooms that make you insecure, declining opportunities, and hiding your gifts. Spiritually, it's running from assignments because they feel unsafe. The trap? Believing that absence equals safety—as if leaving the space also removes the risk.

And then there's freeze. We become paralyzed by the what ifs. In life, that shows up as overthinking every detail until we do nothing at all. Spiritually, it can sound like "I'm just waiting on God," when really we're avoiding the risk that faith requires. The trap here is confusing inactivity with faithfulness, as if standing still equals obedience. But the truth is this: the thorn itself is God's reminder that you are prepared to stand—even if the ground beneath you shakes.

"AND THE BOAT WAS ALREADY A CONSIDERABLE DISTANCE FROM LAND"
MATTHEW 14:24 (NIV)

Here's what I'm learning:

Safety isn't a space.

It's not comfort.

It's not certainty.

It's not control.

Safety is a Person—God.

And sometimes, He's the one letting the storm rage. Not because He wants to see me struggle, but because He wants me to see what's still standing in me—even when everything around me is shaken.

The boat may rock.
The waves may rise.
But if He's in it, I'm still safe.

And when I feel that familiar anxiety creep in—when I'm in a room I can't read, surrounded by people I can't predict, without a script or character to hide behind—I just whisper back to my body:

"I'm not in danger. I'm just uncomfortable right now."

Because falling isn't failing when you're held. And the safest place—even if it feels unstable—is right where He's keeping me.

What I just told you is that there's nowhere to go here—you're in the middle. And the middle is where the water is the deepest, and getting out without protection is a sure way to drown.

So the safest place for you to be... is in the instability of the boat.

Isn't that powerful?!

"I'M 👉 THIS CLOSE TO LOSING MY MIND.. I FEEL LIKE I'M GOING CRAZY...SO MANY THOUGHTS ALL AT ONCE. TURN IT OFF!!"

HEY GOD,

MENTALLY EXHAUSTED

Yea, I'm not gonna lie... I'm over all this.
My brain won't stop.
Bogged down with where I'm supposed to be.
What I'm supposed to be doing.
How I'm supposed to be feeling.
And how that feeling is going to make somebody else feel.
What's the next move?
What's the best move?
How do I even feel?
All I want to know is—where is Joy?
Because it feels like Joy abandoned ship and left every other emotion fighting over the controller.
I'm tired of being genuine and getting played for it.
They say I'm mean.
They say I keep to myself.
But nobody sees how I've been mistreated.
Nobody sees how I've been mishandled.
I gave people the benefit of the doubt.
I tried to be understanding.
And still—I got lied to. I got played.

I don't even want to like or love another person.
My heart is shutting down.
Going cold.
Because when you're nice, people think you're a child's play thing.
And I'm not.
I'm a human.
I have real feelings.
So tell me—who comes to help me sort through these thoughts?
Was it ever real?
What do people really think of me?
The more I think about everything happening to me, around me, the angrier I get.
Why do I miss the one who betrayed me?
Why do I feel sorry for the one who used me?
I don't want any more phone calls.
Leave me alone.

My brain is done.

4.
THE FIGHT OF MY LIFE

In the last chapter, we talked about the first of the two innate human fears—the fear of falling. That one was all about the drop: the terror of losing footing, missing the mark, and being out of control.

But there's a second fear built into our human wiring—the fear of loud noises. And before you dismiss that as something for jumpy toddlers and skittish pets, I want you to think about this: in the middle, the loudest noise isn't always a car backfiring or a thunderclap—it's often the noise in your own head.

That's what makes this fear so dangerous. Because the middle is already disorienting—you're between "what was" and "what's next," navigating without clear answers—and on top of that, the One who sent you here is silent. And in that silence, the voices in your head get louder, your doubts get bolder, and the lies you thought you'd buried start screaming for attention.

This chapter is about that fight—the war that happens when God's silence collides with the noise inside you. And here's the truth: sometimes the loudest noise you'll ever face is not external—it's internal. And if you don't learn how to control it, it will control you.

THE DROP

One day Junee came to me holding his phone like it had barely survived an earthquake. On the outside? Perfect. No cracks, no shattered glass. But the inside told another story—

the screen was glitching, freezing, and scrolling like it was allergic to touch.

"What happened?" I asked.

He shrugged. "I dropped it."

That phone still worked, technically. It could ring. It could text. It could open apps—if you were patient. But the damage on the inside made it frustrating to use.

Junee's solution? "I need a new one."

I fussed. ("We just got this phone!") But here's the confession—I understood him. Because replacing something feels easier than repairing it, especially when the damage is invisible.

And this is exactly what some of us try to do with our faith. We look fine on the outside, but a drop—a betrayal, a loss, a prayer that seemed unanswered—messed with something inside. We still "function": still go to church, still serve, still smile in pictures. But if we're honest, we're glitching inside.

The temptation is to throw it away and start fresh. But damaged doesn't mean dead. Damaged means there's something worth repairing. And your faith has a Manufacturer who knows exactly how to restore what what broke inside you when life dropped you.

"SIMON, SIMON, SATAN HAS ASKED TO SIFT EACH OF YOU LIKE WHEAT.

LUKE 22:31 (NLT)

When I was a kid, I'd watch my grandma bake. She had this silver, mug-shaped gadget with a crank on the side. She'd pour flour in the top, turn the crank, and fine powder would fall out the bottom.

To me, it looked like extra work. I asked why she was doing it, and she said, "Sifting gets the lumps out. It separates what you can use from what you can't."

What I didn't realize is that sifting wasn't gentle. She cranked that handle like she was mad at it. The flour got tossed, scraped, agitated. And whatever didn't meet the standard? Stayed in the mesh and got thrown away.

That's the picture Jesus paints in Luke 22:31–32: "Simon, Simon—Satan has asked to sift you like wheat. But I have prayed for you, that your faith may not fail."

In the Greek, **sift** is σινιάζω (siniázō)—to agitate and shake so intensely on the inside that your faith is overthrown. Not just tested. Overthrown.

The enemy's goal is not just to make your day bad—he wants to run you through a spiritual sifter until you're so frustrated and disoriented that you drop your faith entirely.

But notice Jesus' response: He doesn't pray for Peter's comfort. He doesn't even pray for the shaking to stop. He prays that Peter's faith would not fail. Because your faith is the part of you that outlasts the shaking.

Every war starts because there's something of value. Either someone wants what you have, or they want to stop you from getting what they fear you'll have. That's the core of every fight—possession or prevention.

Wars are fought using different strategies—biological warfare to weaken the body, economic warfare to starve resources, military warfare to dominate territory. But when the battleground is spiritual, Ephesians 6:12 reminds us:

"We wrestle not against flesh and blood, but against principalities, powers, rulers of the darkness of this world, and spiritual wickedness in high places."

That means the person who offended you isn't the enemy. The co-worker who undermines you isn't the enemy. The fight is deeper. The real battle is invisible, and the weapon of choice is often psychological.

Now this is the enemy's true play—he wants your faith. And this is exactly why Jesus called the disciples together when they were busy arguing over irrelevant stuff. While they were debating titles, positions, and petty issues, Jesus basically says: "HEY! Pay attention. Satan has asked for you—to sift you like wheat."

That sift isn't about some old kitchen tool. In the original text, it means to frustrate you so much internally that you overthrow your faith. That's the point—to get you to voluntarily abandon what God said.

CALCULATED WARFARE

It's in this space that depression turns up its volume, anxiety and fear pull out their amps, and disappointment sets up its stage lights.

You start comparing yourself: "Why didn't I get my breakthrough today? Why did it happen for them and not for me?"

Then life throws a punch—bad news, a setback, an unexpected loss. You miss a window of opportunity.

And suddenly, you're standing in the middle of this painful dichotomy:

What God did previously vs. What He said now.

What God promised vs. What I'm actually looking at.

How I feel vs. What I know.

I know what it is to be in this phase of transition:

Where you wake up and don't want to live through another day.

Where you want to smile but tears show up instead.

Where motivation has packed up and left without a forwarding address.

That's the fight of your life—not because of the storm outside you, but because of the war inside you.

My good friend Stephen Chestnut puts it like this: **"Warfare is the contention of two opposing thoughts for the seat of one's mind, because seats are symbolic of authority. Whoever gets the seat determines the course of action… whoever is in the seat has the power."**

Warfare is not random. It's calculated. It studies you—your habits, your patterns, your triggers—and it designs a strategy to move you toward defeat without you even realizing you've been repositioned. Sometimes it doesn't even come with fire and smoke; it comes dressed as "normal life." That's the danger.

When warfare shows up, one of its first moves is to distract you. It may not be with obvious sin, but with stuff—endless tasks, constant noise, small emergencies, or good-but-not-God opportunities. The goal is to keep your eyes off the promise and glued to whatever's urgent in the moment. Then comes the seed of doubt. If the enemy can't take the Word from you, he'll try to take your confidence in it. It's the same line he used in Eden—"Did God really say…?"—because a Word you doubt is a Word you won't act on.

At the same time, he works to drain your joy, because joy is strength. The more your joy runs low, the easier it is to replace gratitude with complaining. Complaining is subtle—it feels like "just being real"—but it's actually the quickest way to change the atmosphere from faith to frustration. Once your joy is low, fatigue sets in. This is where warfare tries to wear you out, not just physically, but emotionally and spiritually. A tired believer prays less, builds less, and resists less. The enemy knows that if he can get you to a place of exhaustion, he won't have to push you out—you'll quit voluntarily.

Offense and division are also key tools in his arsenal. Offense is bait, and once you take it, division is almost inevitable. If he can make you suspicious of people you're called to walk with, he can isolate you from the very relationships meant to help you win. From there, warfare works to steal your focus. The middle is already a battle for attention, so he magnifies lesser things until they feel like the main thing. Now you're busy but not productive—moving, but not advancing. And to seal it all, he amplifies your worry. Worry is simply faith in the wrong direction. It rehearses the worst-case scenario until you start preparing for failure instead of believing for victory.

This is why Ephesians 6:12 is such a wake-up call: "We wrestle not against flesh and blood, but against principalities, powers, rulers of the darkness of this world, and spiritual wickedness in high places." The true fight isn't with people—it's with powers. And if the enemy can keep you fighting people, you'll never confront the spirit behind the problem. This is why you have to learn to identify warfare early, before it takes the driver's seat of your mind and determines where you end up.

The middle is where those opposing thoughts go to war. And psychological warfare is the enemy's favorite tactic—it's the intentional use of what you see and hear to influence what you feel, think, and ultimately do.

WHOSE SEAT IS IT ANYWAY?

Psychological warfare is intentional. It isn't chaos for chaos' sake—it's targeted, calculated, and deeply personal. The enemy tailors it to hit you where you're most vulnerable, aiming to win the battle for your thoughts by wearing down your confidence in God. Spiritually, it plays out in ways that often feel like normal life, but each one is an attempt to gain the seat of authority in your mind.

Sometimes it shows up as emotional abandonment—that deep, aching sense of feeling undesired, left behind, or cut off from the very source you need. In seasons where God feels silent, the enemy will lean in close and whisper, "See? He left you." It's not true—God promises never to leave or forsake you—but if he can get you to believe the lie, he's already halfway to winning the war for your faith.

Other times it comes as separation anxiety—the fear of being detached from the familiar or the uncertainty of stepping into what's next. The disciples felt this when Jesus wasn't physically with them during the storm. The enemy uses it to keep you clinging to comfort instead of following God into calling. It's subtle, but it's powerful, because it convinces you that safety is in the known, when your destiny is in the unknown.

Then there's psychological trauma—the internal injury that convinces you no one will take care of your needs. This is where you find yourself defaulting to fight, flight, or freeze. You fight to control everything, flee from any situation that feels risky, or freeze in hopelessness. Trauma's goal is to make you depend on self-preservation over God's preservation. But the Word is clear: "Be still and know." Stillness isn't surrendering to despair; it's surrendering to His authority.

PTSD keeps you stuck in loops you don't even want to be in—replaying past pain through flashbacks, nightmares, and avoidance. Spiritually, it locks you out of today's opportunities because they resemble yesterday's wounds. The enemy knows that if he can keep you mentally living in an old battle, you'll never engage in your current victory. But God is able to redeem even your memories, turning triggers into testimonies.

Finally, there's BPD—borderline personality disorder—with its cycles of identity uncertainty, chronic emptiness, destructive decisions, and intense emotional swings. Spiritually, the enemy exploits this instability to make you question who you are in Christ. He wants to convince you that your identity is as unstable as your feelings. But the truth is this: your identity in Christ is fixed, sealed, and secure, even when your emotions are not.

This is why psychological warfare is so effective—it doesn't have to destroy you outright; it just has to disorient you enough to hand over the seat of your mind. Once fear is in the driver's seat, faith gets pushed to the back. But you have the authority to choose who sits there.

"ANXIETY... YOU NEED TO LET HER GO"

If you've seen Inside Out 2, you've already had a front-row seat to the chaos that happens inside your own head. One minute, Joy is running the console—everything's bright, hopeful, and full of possibilities. Then Anxiety slides in, pushing every button and warning you about disasters that haven't even happened yet. Sadness follows, wrapping herself in a blanket and slowing everything down. Then Envy pops up, scrolling through someone else's life and making you wonder why yours doesn't look like that. And don't forget Embarrassment, hiding in the corner but ready to shut the whole thing down with one memory from middle school.

Here's the wild part—each of them has a voice, and none of them agree with each other. Joy says, "Go for it!" Anxiety says, "Are you out of your mind?" Sadness whispers, "What's the point?" Envy mutters, "It's better over there," and Embarrassment pleads, "Please, let's not relive that again."

That's not just a cute movie plot—that's Tuesday afternoon in the mind of most believers. Emotions, memories, fears, and insecurities all fighting for the driver's seat, each convinced they're the most qualified to lead. And when you don't know how to assign them to the right place, you'll let whoever's loudest grab the wheel.

But here's the truth: emotions were never meant to be kings—they're advisors. They can speak, but they don't get the seat. The war is won when truth sits in the seat, faith drives, and feelings ride in the back with no access to the GPS. Because left to themselves, feelings will drive you in circles, burn all your fuel, and still not get you to your destination.

GET YOUR MIND BACK

Winning the war in your mind starts with learning to fight feelings with truth. Feelings are real, but they are not always the truth—and if you don't challenge them, they'll lead you somewhere you never wanted to go. This means opening your mouth and speaking God's Word until your soul remembers who's really in charge. You can't just think the truth; you have to say it until it becomes louder than the lies.

From there, you have to secure your inputs. What you hear will always shape what you believe. The voices you allow —whether through people, media, music, or your own inner dialogue—become the architects of your faith or the assassins of it. Guard your ears and your eyes, because they are the gates to your heart.

You also have to close the portals. That means shutting the door on doubt, strife, un-forgiveness, anger, offense, and complaining before they ever take root. Every one of those is an entry point for the enemy to walk right into your thought life and rearrange the furniture. If you keep them open, you'll wonder why your peace keeps leaving.

Rest, prayer, and praise aren't luxuries—they're survival strategies. Sleep is spiritual; it resets your mind and body so you can think clearly. Prayer tunes your frequency back to God's voice, and praise changes the leadership in your heart, reminding your soul that God is still God no matter how you feel.

When the damage feels too deep, return to the Manufacturer. God still repairs in-house, and He honors His own design. Don't run to a source that didn't make you and expect it to know how to fix you. He knows every wire, every connection, every original setting.

Finally, commit to renewing your mind. Real transformation isn't about changing your location or your circumstances; it's about renovating your thought life until it matches what God has already said about you. New surroundings with the same old thinking will get you the same old results. But a renewed mind will produce a renewed life—even in the same place.

If you're in the fight of your life, remember: your faith is not failing—it's being fortified. Jesus is praying for you. And when you come through this (and you will), you'll be able to strengthen someone else.

Truth gets the seat. Faith drives. Feelings ride in the back —no aux cord.

You're going to make it to the other side of this. Say it out loud. Your mind needs to hear your mouth.

DEAR GOD

LETTERS FROM "THE MIDDLE"

"I HAVE FAITH... BUT I ALSO HAVE FEELINGS. WHERE CAN I GO TO DUMP MY FEELINGS WITHOUT MY FAITH BEING QUESTIONED?"

THESE ARE NOT THE "AFTER" STORIES. THESE ARE THE RIGHT NOW PRAYERS.

There are some prayers that don't fit neatly into a worship song or a Sunday morning testimony. They're messy. Unpolished. Uncomfortable to say out loud.

These aren't the prayers you post about. These are the ones you whisper in the car on the way home. The ones you write in your notes app at 2 AM. The ones that sound less like "Our Father" and more like "Are You even listening?"

The truth is—God can handle all of it. He can handle our trembling faith, our side-eye questions, our moments of silence, and even our "I'm mad at You" phases.

This section is exactly that: raw, unfiltered letters from the middle. Not the victory lap. Not the "I made it through" recap. But the messy, foggy, in-between—where you can't see the shore and the waves are still high.

Some of these letters are mine. Others belong to people who were brave enough to be honest. You'll hear desperation, anger, surrender, confusion, and even humor. Because the middle isn't just hard—it's complicated.

As you read them, I hope two things happen:

You see yourself in these pages and realize you're not the only one feeling what you're feeling.

You feel the permission to write your own letter to God— uncut, unedited, un-preached.

DEAR GOD,

We need to talk.
God, my God—
Where are You?
Where am I?
Where is the Presence You promised in my time of trouble?
These were the questions that haunted me, chiseling away at the little bit of faith I could muster up.
Like Abraham, You called me away from home, sent me into foreign lands with nothing but a word to stand on.
No familiar faces.
No step by step plan.
Just a small bag of belongings and a lot of hope.
I left everything I knew—my safety, my comfort, my roots. I traded the comfort of the familiar
for the future You had planned for me.
I gave up the little I had for the promises of all You had in store. I laid down security to chase after something sacred.
And yet... I came up short.
Teary eyes and empty hands were all I had.
Time and again, I'd touch breakthrough
only to break down. I'd get a taste of progress but tribulation was never far behind.
The future felt impossible.
Purpose became a puzzle full of missing pieces.
Even the promises began to lose their shine.
And if this was the price of obedience, I wanted a refund.

No exchange.
No substitutions.
Just release me from this cycle of suffering.
But then—in the stillness between despair and desperation—You spoke.
You reminded me:
Your promises still stand.
You cannot lie.
You never leave.
You never left.
It was my pain that clouded Your presence,
my obsession of the future that blurred Your nearness in the here and now.
You were waiting for me all along.
For me to look up.
To let go.
To let You.

Let You lead.
Let You hold.
Let You order my steps.
Let you guide and be God.
And in the terror of the night, You took my trembling hands and whispered to my aching heart:
"My grace will carry you from suffering to glory."
You reminded me that You're not any less God in the storm than You are in the calm.
You're God in the beginning.
God in the middle.
God at the end.

And because of Your grace, the middle didn't consume me.
You were there all along.
Still God.
Still good.
Still mine.
And you are still here.
Still carrying. Still calling.
Still making it all work for my good.
~ YOUR CHILD

DEAR GOD,

Forgiveness.
I haven't forgiven her
Laid out all the charges.
And granted her acquittal.
I haven't forgiven her.
I kept thinking danger is knocking at my door that if I don't stand guard I let the monster in.
I haven't forgiven her.
I've tried to forget.
Thinking that's the way for things to be easier but with every good moment I'm on guard.
I don't know what to do with her.
I'd rather......
I'm fighting the dream of a happy ending
Teardrops fade in the sand as a new life begins.
I hope for her.
Thinking that there will be better days where I respect her and feel her safety
Where I know no harm will come against me
Where rehearsed hurt doesn't comfort me
I release her.
Is it really that easy?
Is the gospel really true?
If Jesus could save a wretch like me could I really forgive you?
Does it even matter if it happens? Will it just be me stomaching all the hurt?
Will you do it again?

Will giving you access to me work?
You've done so many wrongs.
70 times 7 doesn't seem to make it right.
Should I let go of the pain?
Is forgiveness/ redemption in sight?
I love you mom. God knows I do.
Love keeps no record of wrongs.
Love is patient. Love is kind. Love I know will forever remain strong.
In movies love always wins. In the bible it remains true. So forgiveness must be possible. This exchange from me to you.
This is easy. No it ain't...to trust and let go.
But I love you and I trust that God will let me know.
He will shield me. Protect me.
He claimed the lover of my soul.
Lord help me to know I gave my heart to you alone.
So, because its yours not hers. Do you promise to keep it safe?
This is a gift you gave so tenderly not mine to keep close.
So. to...day. For. you...
I forgive her repeatedly.
~ YOUR CHILD

DEAR GOD,

WHO GIVES ME PERMISSION TO CRY?

My thoughts are sporadic—scattered everywhere.

I feel so heavy.

I don't know if this weight is all mine or if it's the empath in me, but I don't feel inspired anymore. At all. If I'm honest, I feel like I'm about to break.

I want to cry… but I don't know how.

Sounds crazy, right?

I remember being younger, standing in church, and my aunt making fun of me because I couldn't cry. Not even in worship. She said I was trying too hard to push out tears but nothing came out. And maybe she was right… because even now, I can feel the tears welling up in the corners of my eyes, but they never fall.

Today, I hate my journey.

I appreciate it, I know it has purpose, I know it shaped me—but I hate it. I feel ruined by it.

My love life—nonexistent as it is—feels ruined by this journey. And I fear it always will be. I feel like I'll forever be stained, judged, and misunderstood by it.

And as bad as I want to cry, I can't.

Maybe it stems from my childhood. I used to cry a lot, but after so many "Stop crying like a little girl, boys don't cry!" moments… I think my body believed it. So now, even as a grown man who's made breakthroughs, I still feel ruined by what I went through.

Who gives me permission to cry now?

Every time I want to, there's this strong voice wired into me saying: "Nope. Stop that."
God, why did You let them do that to me?
Now everybody wants me to show emotion. To not be so nonchalant. But the moment I do, my manhood gets questioned. And if I don't let people in, I'm a jerk.
So which one is it?
Because right now, I feel like I'm about to implode.
I need help.
Life isn't helping either. Everything around me just points me back to pit stops on my journey. So many people contributed to my ruin, but not many are willing to contribute to my healing.
I feel alone.
And while I know I'm not ruined... I still feel like I'm on the clearance rack. Like everybody's rushing to the shiny new things while I get passed over.
It sucks being me sometimes.
I have worth too.
I'm good too.
But who wants damaged goods?
Your Word says You bottle up tears.
Well, I guess You don't have any from me, huh?
Many pray for You to rescue them...
But God, I just want to cry.
Can You help me with that?
Or am I going to stay bottled up until the day I die?
Because honestly... I just want to know—
what do I have to do to cry?
~ YOUR CHILD

DEAR GOD,

Oh Lord, You are the author of my story—a story I can't skip ahead to read. You are my anchor in a storm I didn't choose. You did. And I'm trying to remember that in the middle of it.

Sometimes I have fainting spells when I pause and compare where I am to what You've shown me. I get disheartened when it looks like my promise won't come to pass. I grow weary at the thought of living out what Rita Louise Watson's mama called "singing your shoulda, coulda, wouldas" in Sister Act II.

What if I'm building a career that won't yield much fruit? I'm over thirty now. What if this abstinence journey was just a scheme that Todd set up to leave me childless and husband-less? What if I'm not as great as people think I am? And if I am, wouldn't there be some fruit by now?

Yet right in the middle of my lament, You slip treasures of hope into my hands. You send provision in unexpected ways. In famine, you send nutrients through ravens, and it's just enough to keep me holding tighter.

I hate the valley, Lord. Everyone does. It's the stretch between peaks that feels like the drop. But then I read about Jehoshaphat in 2 Chronicles 20. You sent word through a messenger that his enemies had teamed up to wage war. But You told him not to fear because the battle was Yours, not his. And on the fourth day, they gathered in the Valley of Blessing, which is named that because they praised and thanked You there. It's still called that today.

And something in me stirred. Because it's in the valley—right in the middle—that You give us the tools to live high on the mountain. So although I'm in a waiting season, I lift my hands and pray, "If this is my season to be in the valley, at least make it the Valley of Blessing."

The middle doesn't have to be sorrowful because I know where I'm headed. You didn't tell me how long I'd be here, but that's where faith comes in. The God of my mountains is also the Lord of my valleys.

So I choose to adjust my posture. My hands may get scraped, my breath may grow short, my knees may buckle—but I trust You. You, O Lord, know my end from my beginning. I will not let my heart be troubled. Like David, I declare, "I would have fainted unless I had believed to see the goodness of the Lord in the land of the living" (Psalm 27:13).

The middle sometimes hurts. But I will not despise it. Because in the middle, You shape me. And when the promise comes, I'll look back and declare this middle ground as holy ground.

To the only wise God, my Savior: let me not just find You in the end. Help me remember You ordained the middle. And for that, I thank You.

~ YOUR CHILD

DEAR GOD,

I don't know what You're doing.
I just know how I feel.
And while I know my feelings are valid—but not the truth—that doesn't comfort me right now. Because I'm feeling them real bad.
I'm at my wits' end again.
And yes, I've been here before, but this fresh wave feels like it's hijacking my memory and robbing my hope.
I'm tired of being strong.
I'm tired of fighting to see light at the end of the tunnel.
I'm tired of setbacks.
Tired of disappointments.
I really want to quit everything.
I'm not asking for a life without trouble.
But a reprieve? A break? A season of wins? That would help.
You know better than me—I don't want to play God, I don't want to take Your place. I just want to be honest about where I am. Right now, it's very hard to see the light.
Hope feels like a carrot dangling in front of my face.
Why keep chasing something I'm not getting closer to?
It feels like time wasted.
I'm moody. Erratic. Angry. Frustrated. Disappointed.
And yet—something in me won't let me walk away.
That pisses me off.
I want to unsubscribe.
I didn't even want to wake up today.

I felt attacked in my sleep—so I know this is bigger than me, bigger than my feelings. The weight of the attack makes me believe something is up...
But God, if You don't help me, I'm going to die.
And while I want to live, I don't want to live like this.
So please... help me.
I am so tired.
I really just want to give up.
Why has my life been like this?
What's the point? Is it even worth it?
Is fulfillment a lie?
Am I reaching for the wrong thing?
Is it bad to want what You showed me?
Because what You showed me and where I am right now don't match.
Is this how Joseph felt in the pit?
Is this what David felt running for his life?
I'm trying to believe this is all on course—that seasons change.
But this one feels permanent.
Loss after loss. Heartache after heartache.
God, I just need a break.
Some good things to happen.
I'm under so much pressure.
It's hard to move forward.
I'm tired of being let down.
I'm tired of grieving.
Lord, I'm tired.
And I don't know how much more I can take.

Part of me feels bad for even feeling like this.
Because I know You're real.
So why do I want to walk away?
I've seen You use me to bring life and hope to others...
But when will it happen for me?
I have so many questions.
I'm trying not to stress, but I can't help it.
I'm losing my will to fight.
I'm right on the edge of saying, "Forget it all."
Am I still just trying to control things?
~ YOUR CHILD

DEAR GOD,

So often it is hard for me to tell you the honest truth of how I feel. I know that you know what I'm thinking—after all, you are omniscient—but it feels different when I say it. Once it's out there, I can't take it back, and you see how I "truly" feel. Why is that, Lord? I know you already know my heart! Yet I find myself judging my feelings when you haven't.

The truth is, the middle is hard. Right now, I'm navigating the tension between my desire for financial security and the calling to help build a church from the ground up. This is not what I envisioned when I thought you would use me in a different church role. I feel like I'm constantly walking a tightrope, trying to balance my faith with the practical realities of life. I want to be mature in my faith, but sometimes I just want to roll around on the floor and cry, overwhelmed by the weight of responsibility.

I remember a time when I was drowning in financial chaos—my credit cards maxed out, my account perpetually negative, and rent looming over me like a dark cloud. Just when I thought I was over that hump, things seemed to get better for a while. But now, as we prepare to launch this new church, I feel the pressure building again. It's not as dire as before, but the stress is still palpable, reminding me of those tough days. I find myself repeating those moments, feeling the anxiety creep back in, whispering doubts about whether I can really do this.

How do I balance the principles I know to be true about you, like your perfect timing and your care for my needs, with the reality of my financial struggles? Can I truly trust in your provision while feeling the weight of uncertainty? Does the way I feel cancel out the moments when I'm striving to walk out your principles? I know you want to use me, but I can't lie and say I don't hope and pray you bless me through this process.

I often wonder if my dreams are too big for my reality. I think back to the moments when I felt your presence so strongly, guiding me, but now it feels like I'm lost in a fog. I question whether I'm on the right path and I have what it takes to stay consistent.

Sometimes I feel like I'm standing in the middle of a storm, trying to hold on to faith while the winds of doubt howl around me. I want to help others, to see my pain have purpose, but Lord, please assure me that there will be a silver lining at the end of this journey. I long for the day when I can share my story of struggle and victory, to encourage others who find themselves in their own middle moments.

Yet, in this chaos, I also want to be honest with you about my fears. I worry that I'm not enough, that my efforts won't yield the fruit I hope for. I'm reminded of Philippians 4:19: "And my God will meet all your needs according to the riches of his glory in Christ Jesus." How can I hold on to this promise when my needs feel so overwhelming?

Help me to trust you more, even when my faith feels fragile. Teach me how to lean into you when the ground feels unsteady beneath my feet. Show me how to embrace the process, knowing that growth often happens in the waiting. I bring my raw emotions to you, unfiltered and real. The chaos feels overwhelming at times, and it's hard to see past the immediate struggles.

I lay it all before you, trusting that you are with me in this journey. I'm learning to be open about my feelings, even when they feel messy and complex. Thank you for holding my heart, even when it feels heavy and burdened. I cling to the hope that you are crafting something beautiful out of this season of waiting and uncertainty.

As I look ahead, I dream of a time when I can stand firm in my faith, confident in your provision. I envision a thriving community built on love and hope, where my struggles become the foundation for others' strength. I trust that you are weaving all of this together for good, even when I can't see it.

~ YOUR CHILD

DEAR GOD,

I thought You said You were my friend. I thought You said You cared about me. I thought You said You loved me. This doesn't feel like care or love or even consideration most days now. I'm at, probably, the most pivotal time in my life. I DON'T EVEN WANT TO BE HERE AT THAT. YOU chose this for me. YOU placed me here. I never wanted this. I knew I couldn't handle it. I still can't handle this. Where are you even? Why am I even wasting any more time waiting on You. Or calling for You. How many days have I called You now?? How many tears have I dropped? My real dad won't answer the phone and to make matters worse, You as my Heavenly Father are also choosing to ignore me. You don't see me in pain? You don't see me falling apart? You don't see me? What did I do? I'm sorry. I'm so sorry. I repent. Sincerely, I repent. I just need help. I'm so tired. I'm exhausted. I've never felt this alone before. You chose the hardest time in my life to leave.. You let me agree to Your will, knowing You'd just sit back while I crumble underneath the weight of the decision YOU made for my life.. why would You do that? I thought I knew You. This isn't who I know You to be. God, I --- This isn't how I want to feel. I'm so angry. At You. At Me. This isn't who You made me to be. I'm losing faith in You. The point of trying this hard to stay by Your side is getting more and more unclear. It's like You're just watching everything worsen. And You have the power to stop it. You have the strength to push it back. It feels like You're not doing anything but waking me up every morning and putting breath in me. At this point I can't even decide if that's a blessing or just another part of this punishment or is it just cruelty.. You've never just been cruel. You've never left me.. You've never turned Your back on me... Please turn back. Please just see me.. I'm sorry. I'm not even faithful enough to be this upset. If I were to be honest this is the most I've talked to You consistently.. is that why?? I repent. Please don't use my baby to prove that I need you. I know I need You. God please, I can't watch him suffer because of me. God please. Jesus please. Jesus please. Jesus please. Please. I can't do this without You. I'm too weak. I was never strong enough to do this life without You, but especially now. Jesus, my heart. Something is off. There's a darkness and I'm afraid. Please don't harden my heart towards You. I don't want to lose my son. I know I don't always do right. I know I haven't done what You told me to do. Ugh! You probably don't even hear all this. This isn't how You taught me to come to You or ask for You. God, Jesus, Savior.... Father, save me. I am trying to trust You. I am trying to follow You, but I don't even see the markings of the direction You've gone.. If You're still here. If You still can hear me at all. I need You. I'm crying to You from the pit of distress, I need You to hear me. I need You to answer. Please.

~ YOUR CHILD.

DEAR GOD,

Hey, we need to talk.
I've been thinking about life where I sometimes reside emotionally and whew, it sucks.
I feel like I've taken every obstacle on the chin, never complained about it, stood strong IN it. SO WHEN DOES IT STOP??!! Like, is this really what it's going to be forever? I'm just going to be strong ALL of my life? WOW. So much trust. 🤐
On the worst of these days, I'll cry the entire day. My poor husband. He prays 15x a day all because of me! I can see an article, hear from one of "his" relatives and my heart breaks all over again. Can't believe this has to be added to my story. Cant believe I'm constantly having to check myself to see if there's any hate in my heart because people tell me it's supposed to be there, so i can be delivered from it.
But it's not there.
There's no hate there. There's disappointment, there's sadness, but surprisingly, no hate. There's love there. There's hope and there's life. And because I choose to hold on to what's positive, I'll respect when I'm sad and heartbroken, but when the day ends, I will always rest in the fact that I know You love me. I know You care about me. My lived experience does not indicate an absence of You.

And I'm thankful for that, because I'm being exactly what You designed me to be.
Complex, but grateful for it all.
~ YOUR CHILD

DEAR GOD,

I'm trying. I really am. I trust You—I keep telling myself I do. I believe Your Word. I know it's real. I've seen You come through before, with my own eyes. I've watched miracles happen. So I know You're able.

But right now... this season is breaking me. My faith feels like it's hanging by a thread. I'm anxious, I'm worried, I'm tired. Some days I don't even want to get out of bed. Some days I feel nothing—like I'm just floating outside my own body, watching life pass me by.

I've shown up for so many people. I've put others on. I've lifted them when they needed it. But when it's me in need, when I'm the one drowning, it feels like no one is there. And it hurts. Your Word says a brother is born for adversity, but God, where are mine?

I don't know what You're trying to teach me. I don't know what You want from me. If I need to surrender something, show me—because I don't know how much longer I can do this. Every time I think it can't get worse, it does. Every time I think I've finally caught my breath, something else knocks me down. I'm tired, God. I'm worn out.

And what breaks me most is this: I pray for others, and I see You move. I celebrate their wins. I watch them walk in joy and purpose. But when I pray for me, when I cry out for me, it feels like silence. I feel forgotten. Left behind. Numb.

God, I know I haven't been perfect with what You've given me. I've made mistakes. But I've always believed You for the impossible. And I need the impossible now. Not tomorrow, not "someday"—now. Restore my joy. Bring back my peace. Put fire in me again. Give me a reason to wake up excited about purpose again.

I know life isn't all easy. I know following You isn't about comfort. But I also know You didn't put me here to suffer like this. So please—when will this season end? Because I'm close to giving up. And You're the only thing holding me here.

I don't even have tears left most days. I'm just empty. But even from that emptiness, all I can say is this: God, I need You. And I need You now.

~ YOUR CHILD

DEAR GOD,

    I've been receiving constant reminders that I can either pray about it or worry about it — I can't do both. And honestly, that's the tension I've been sitting in for months now. I feel like I'm stuck in the middle of so many unknowns, unexpected transitions, and waves of anxiety. It's exhausting. I know I'm not in control, but still... everything that's happening (and not happening) weighs on me every single day. I can't help but wonder — why do You have me sitting here in the middle? What am I supposed to be learning? And how long will I be here?

The day after I found out I was losing my job this year, my devotional told me: "Your setback could be a setup for what's next. Lean into the faithfulness of God." That message landed right in the middle of one of the busiest, most chaotic times of my year.

I told myself everything happens for a reason, and that helped me stay a little optimistic even while I was hurting. But Father, I can't lie — I was so confused.

You know my heart. I've tried to live my life with purity, with generosity, and with respect. I give back to my community not for recognition, but because that's what You've called me to do. I give You honor for every single blessing in my life. So why this season? Why now? Why

do I have to carry something that feels so heavy and uprooting, especially
when I wasn't ready? I don't like to question You, but I found myself angry, Lord.

Angry... and yet, still sitting.

Being still with You is one of the hardest things I've ever had to do. It means letting go of my own control and putting my full trust in You — even when I don't understand. It
means leaning into the discomfort instead of running from it, and believing that somewhere in all of this, You're creating new normals I haven't seen yet. What I've been learning — and what I'm still learning — is that I can't stop living while I wait. Even in the hard seasons, I have to hold onto the things that bring me joy, the things that make me feel like ME. Lord, my flesh wanted to shut down, to give in to negativity. But I kept fighting to stay aligned with where I know You want me — seated, but prepared.

God, even in the middle of this space, I want to say thank You. Thank You for being with me through the waves of emotion, the uncertainty, and the prayers that feel like they go unanswered. That saying, "If you want to make God laugh, tell Him your plans" —has been so true in my life lately. I had plans, and they came to a screeching halt. I set new goals, thinking they'd move me forward, and those didn't work out either. For a while, it felt like You weren't listening. But really, You were waiting for me to give You more than my trust in just the good times. You wanted me to trust You in the moments when I felt completely lost.

And Lord, that's where I am. The middle. It's hard, it's humbling, it's stretching me in ways that sometimes feel unbearable. But I also know You meet me here. So even in this, I'm choosing to trust You. We're never given more than we can bear, and you'll never take us to a place and leave us alone. I'll be here when it's time...

~ YOUR CHILD

DEAR GOD,

Can we talk? Now, by no means am I cursing you or charging you foolishly. I just need to pour out my raw emotion. I'm not accusing you, and I'm not even calling this truth—this is just how I feel, unfiltered and unsanitized.

I read a question in the book of Job that I want to throw back to you. You asked the enemy, "Have you considered my servant?" And God, with no disrespect, I want to pose that same question: Have you considered me? Have you considered my heart? Have you considered the aftermath of the frequent blows? I know you know what you're doing, and I believe the scripture that says you care for us. But what are you doing with the care? You have all power to shift and turn things, yet you let them stay the same. Have you not considered the damaging effect this has on me?

You made me, you know me better than I know myself. I'm still discovering who I am, but I've learned one thing: being considered matters to me. My heart breaks when I'm not considered. I'm not a difficult person. I don't ask for much. I just want to be okay. I don't need the biggest house, the fanciest cars, or designer clothes—I'm good with hoodies and sweatpants. I'm not chasing advancement to flex; I just want to help people. So why is it so hard for me?

When Granny Bobbie was diagnosed with cancer and seemed to be gone within two weeks, I begged you to heal her. Nothing happened. When I fasted, prayed, and believed for my cousin Bobo to recover from his heart condition, he still died. I'll give you Big Mama—she was up in age, and while my heart wasn't ready, I can move on from that. But then there was Lil James—the one person who truly saw me, encouraged me, and stood in my corner. He dies in a motorcycle accident while talking to you? And then Anjelica and Kaylia—who you had me prophesy to and believe for—they're gone too. At my grandmother's funeral, I pleaded with you for no more loss. Five and a half months later, Aunt Netta—same hospital, same tower. Death after death. Loss after loss. God, it feels like you're more interested in breaking my heart than mending it. What's up with that?

Do I deserve this? I know I'm not perfect, but I'm not asking for anything unrealistic. Just a break. A season of good things. Losing friends, loved ones, and then the cherry on top—losing my job in the middle of it all. Now I'm working a more stressful job for less pay, struggling to make ends meet. I can't fix anything, do anything, or even dream about a vacation—I haven't had one since 2018. Why gift me with the weight and responsibility of helping others only to leave me rejected and empty? Why does everything I pour into seem to crumble?

I'm tired, God. This isn't me coming at you wrong—this is just how I feel. It sucks to encourage others and come home to cry. It sucks to pour myself out for people and still feel rejected. To show up great and be treated as mediocre. To love and be betrayed. To work hard and still have so little to show for it. HAVE YOU CONSIDERED ME? And if so, at what point will you consider it to be enough? How long does my heart have to ache and break? I'm not asking for a trouble-free life, just a break.

The most-asked question in my life right now is: Josh, how are you? How are you feeling?

The truth?

I don't want to die.

But I don't want to live like this either.

I'm tired of being here like this. Tired of people clapping for me when I feel like sh*t. Is it weird that I hate and love my life at the same time? Is this life—being uncomfortable, stretched, hurt, lied to—all to be "comforted" by empty words?

"It's gon' be alright." Yeah? When? And for how long? "Be strong." Man, I've been strong all my life. I'm tired of being strong. Being strong got me where? Let me give being weak a try.

What actually changes now? I've prayed. I've cried. I've coped in both right and wrong ways. My dreams are blurry, my expectations are in hell, and my reality is excessively stressful and heartbreaking. I'm tired of getting my hopes up just to be let down. I don't want sensationalism—I want truth. Does it actually get better, or is that just what people say to keep me going?

Truth is, I'm dog tired. Tired of smiling when the truth in my face makes people uncomfortable. Tired of performing because people need me, all the while I'm not well. Tired of losing, tired of empty words, tired of making ends meet, tired of pushing, tired of not settling—just tired of trying.

I'm 30+, hating life but loving the people I get to do life with. I'm only staying because I don't want the people I love to feel the weight of the loss I carry.

Truth is, I WANT TO DIE. But I want to live too. I'm conflicted, angry, hurt, betrayed. In all of this, I still have a sliver of hope whispering that the future I've seen is still possible—that better is real.

After all this, the question in my head is: What the hell do I do? Keep living and hope for the best, or die trying? I'm tired. Haven't I learned enough? Isn't my character developed yet? Can I get a time frame? How long will my heart bleed? I just want to be a light—I didn't know I'd have to live in darkness to be seen.

I love for things to make sense, and none of this does. How do I want to end it all and keep living at the same time?

Working a job that doesn't bring satisfaction, just so I can lay my head down safely at night. Moving through life on muscle memory, with spaces of time unaccounted for because I've mentally checked out. Is this really life? Why can't I just live subconsciously—just be there?

My mind races faster than it processes and quicker than my thumbs can move. From the moment my eyes open to the moment they close, my brain is racing: What about this? How is this going to work? Do I stop loving to lessen the pain, or keep loving and brace for the next loss? What happens when it comes too soon?

Am I breakable? Because I feel like I am. I feel like one more thing—like a flat tire—could be the thing that snaps me. How much can I take? Can that measurement be reduced? I know everybody has their lot, but man it, this is a lot. Too much or not yet? That's the question my soul keeps asking. I'm walking on eggshells, cautiously, wondering if I'm next to break.

These are my thoughts in a matter of minutes. Imagine a day's worth. I'm depleted, mentally exhausted, in pain, in fear, not happy—just trying not to crumble.

How am I? This is how I'm feeling. Everything in me recoils at that question. I know people don't ask it to harm me, but every time they do, this is what flashes through my head.

Everything in question gets questioned. I feel guilty for even feeling my feelings. I just want to know: What can be done about how I'm feeling? Because it looks like I have two options: live or die. Quit or keep going. At any given time of the day, I'm at some point on that spectrum.

I would love to feel safe. Constantly. I don't want to feel like a burden. I want to experience the joy I bring to others.

I have a lot of questions—maybe even concerns. But the biggest one is this: Does Josh want to live or die? Depending on the moment, both seem like the right answer. The timing of the choice is the tricky part.

I'm just Josh. I'm not strong. I'm not the version people made me out to be. I'm just a man having to make a decision multiple times a day. And this is what runs through my head: Do you know what it feels like to drown, never get saved, but not die? It's torture. And while they clap because I've written books and achieved things, I'm sitting on my bed, crying, trying to breathe, trying not to give in to impulse.

I don't want to die right now. But I don't want to live like this either.

I kinda feel like Jeremiah.

This is my Lamentation.

I wrote this in January of 2023, in the depth of my grief. And here I am in January of 2025, still feeling the same way. WHY DO I FEEL LIKE I'M STUCK in this never-ending cycle of being broken? WILL IT EVER END? Will it ever be worth it? Or is my living really in vain?

I'm just a man who wants to be considered entirely.

So, God, have you considered me?

~ YOUR CHILD

5.
WHAT'S THIS...WHO DAT?!

My niece Bella Grace is my pride and joy. To know me is to know that I love kids—and not just kids, but smart kids. Bella is that child. She's gifted, energetic, and musical to the core. Just like her mom and me, she'll break out in a song without hesitation. Recently, she discovered Alexa, and now every time she sees me, her request is the same: "Alesha, please play Baby Shark." It's the cutest thing.

She's also obsessed with Halloween. Anytime she spots a pumpkin, she starts singing "Trick or Treat, Happy Halloween!" That's just who she is—songs and joy are her language.

One weekend, I was at her house, and she wanted me to take her outside. Now listen, I am not the outdoors type. I think nature is prettiest on a postcard, not in person. But anything for Bella. So out we went. She had me running around, rolling in the grass, doing cartwheels. And I finally told her, "Bella, Uncle don't do grass." Which is true—because I don't like snakes or any other creatures that hide in the blades.

Her response? She stopped what she was doing, threw her little arms up, and yelled in the cutest way: "I'm not scared!" It's one of her favorite lines from her top-five hit, *Going on a Bear Hunt*. We ended up having a whole concert outside, singing and laughing. But here's the irony: she was only bold enough to declare "I'm not scared" while she was in my arms. The moment I tried to put her down, she clung tighter and fear showed up again.

That's the nature of fear. It isn't always logical—it's relational. Fear shrinks when you feel safe, and safety changes your language.

Now truthfully, I've never considered myself a scary person. I actually like scary things. The scarier the movie, the better. There are only two I refuse to watch: Candyman—never happening—and one Freddy Krueger movie, New Nightmare, that traumatized me as a kid. Everything else? Let's go. To me, "fake" scary doesn't scare me.

But real fear? Real fear gets me every time.

And here's what I've learned: all fear is rooted in a lack of information. Fear feeds on what you don't know.

I can only remember two times in my life when I was genuinely afraid—and both of them happened in the dark.

The first was when I was about ten or eleven. I'd be in my room, playing Nintendo 64, and every night around 7 or 8 p.m., I felt a presence. Not just a vibe—it was like something entered the room. Nothing moved, nothing shook, but I felt it. And it terrified me.

So every night, at that exact time, I'd turn off my game and go find my mom or sister. I never admitted I was afraid—because I was too much of a "G" for that—but the truth is I was scared. I always loved my space, but during that season, I'd sneak into my mom's or sister's bed just to feel safe. I knew it was something spiritual, because it stopped when I started sleeping with my Bible under my pillow. After that, it never came back.

The second time is almost funny. I was staying at my aunt's house, and my cousins—professional tormentors—decided to put on The Texas Chainsaw Massacre. I was fine until my uncle kept repeating, "This is a true story." Freddy Krueger never scared me because he was fictional, but Leatherface? A man with a chainsaw? That felt possible.

On the ride home, I stared out the window the whole way, convinced I was next. Why? Because my closet at home had a small hole in the wall and an access door in the floor to the crawlspace under the house—just like the movie. I wanted to move out that night. Only years later did I learn the "real" killer had died or been in prison long before I was born. Context mattered.

And that's the point: fear grows in the dark because information is missing. The less you know, the more your imagination runs wild. And apparently, I'm not alone in this. Studies show that about 75% of children are afraid of the dark. Even more surprising? Roughly 50% of adults are too. Why? Because darkness doesn't just hide what is—it triggers your imagination about what might be lurking there.

That's why fear isn't always about reality. Fear often isn't about what is—it's about what might be.

SHORTLY BEFORE DAWN JESUS WENT OUT TO THEM, WALKING ON THE LAKE. WHEN THE DISCIPLES SAW HIM WALKING ON THE LAKE, THEY WERE TERRIFIED. "IT'S A GHOST," THEY SAID, AND CRIED OUT IN FEAR.

MATTHEW 14:25-26 (NIV)

I've heard this saying all my life: "It's always darkest right before dawn."

At first, it sounds like just another cliché, but when you look at it through the lens of Scripture, it carries weight. Matthew 14 says that when Jesus came walking on the water, it was during the fourth watch of the night. That's about 3 a.m.—the darkest part of the night, right before the sun even thinks about rising.

Picture this: the disciples had already been fighting a storm for hours. The winds were against them, the waves were crashing, and they were exhausted. Physically drained. Emotionally tapped out. Mentally done. And then, in the middle of that chaos and in the pitch of night, they see something moving on the water.

Now, let's be real—when you're already tired, stressed, and surrounded by darkness, your mind doesn't automatically jump to faith. It jumps to fear. And that's exactly what happened. The disciples immediately cried out, "It's a ghost!"

But here's the lesson: the darkest hour is when your sight is most limited, and your imagination fills in the gaps. And when your imagination runs the show, it almost always paints the worst-case scenario. The disciples weren't seeing clearly—they were seeing through fear. And fear will always cause you to mislabel what's right in front of you.

I don't know how many of you have ever been on a cruise before, but I've been on a number of them, and the Lido deck gave me a whole new understanding of why the disciples panicked that night.

I was on a family cruise right after graduating high school. I was eighteen, and the night was young for me. I had just left the teenage club on the Carnival ship—it was lit. I turned the boat upside down, made some friends, got some numbers, lived my best life. Afterward, a group of us went to the Lido deck, which is the late-night spot for food and ice cream. See, after the formal dinner, your food options get real slim. You can't just hit up McDonald's—you're stuck with what's on the ship. So we grabbed ice cream and decided to head to the railing to talk and laugh.

What I saw next changed me.

I leaned over the railing, and it was pitch black. I'm talking nothing. No horizon. No glimmer of light on the waves. Just darkness that felt alive. It was like staring into the abyss. I could literally see nothing. And in that moment, a thought hit me hard: If anyone fell over, they'd be falling for a very long time.

Here's the crazy part: the boat itself was lit up. Lights everywhere. Bright enough to feel like daytime. The moon was in the sky, glowing in its fullness. But none of that mattered. The waters below stayed dark, untouched, unbothered by the light above them.

That's when I realized something the disciples must have felt. Being surrounded by light doesn't mean you see clearly. You can be in a place filled with activity, joy, and energy, and still feel like you're staring into nothing. The dark waters don't respond to the glow of the ship or the shine of the moon—they remind you of your smallness, your helplessness, and the fact that sometimes, no matter how much light is around you, you're still left with the unknown beneath you.

That's what fear does in the dark. It convinces you that the abyss is bigger than your God. It makes you forget that even when it looks like nothing, He's still there, hovering.

WHAT ARE WE?!: THE DANGER OF MISLABELING

I'll never forget one of my past relationships—it taught me more about perspective than I ever expected. I've been single for a long time, since 2017 to be exact, but back then, I found myself in what started out as a really good thing. We began as friends, and it was amazing. We laughed constantly, talked on the phone for hours, spent time together without the pressure of expectation. It was light, it was joyful, and it was easy. Naturally, when you're having such a good time with someone, you think the next step is to make it official. So we did. We went from "just friends" to "boyfriend and girlfriend."

Whew, Chile... why did we do that?

Almost overnight, everything shifted. The laughs turned into arguments. The joy was replaced with resentment. The carefree ease became heavy, complicated, and tense. I'll never forget one argument where she got so mad at me that she actually threw car keys at my head. And me—being the nice guy that I am—I stood there shocked. (And yes, she threw them hard.) We're cool now, but at the time it was rough. Closer to the end of that relationship, we went to IHOP, and I told her straight up: "As my friend, I love you. You're amazing. But as my girlfriend… it's a no for me. I can't stand you."

It sounded harsh, and she told me I was the meanest person walking the earth, but what I was really trying to point out was this: when we were just friends, things were relaxed, life-giving, and fun. But once we slapped the "boyfriend/girlfriend" label on it, the dynamic shifted entirely. And it's because what you call a thing determines how you behave toward it.

That's the principle: You'll always mismanage what you mislabel.

If you call it the wrong thing, you'll handle it the wrong way.

And this doesn't just apply to relationships. It shows up in every area of life. When you mislabel a season, you'll mismanage it. If you call your help a hindrance, you'll push away the very people God sent to lift you. If you call your process a punishment, you'll resist the very growth God is trying to produce in you. If you call the storm an enemy, you'll miss the Savior walking toward you in the middle of it.

That's what happened to the disciples in Matthew 14. They mislabeled Jesus as a ghost. They let fear and darkness redefine their perception of Him. And because they called Him the wrong thing, they were about to handle Him the wrong way—by running from their answer.

How you see a thing determines how you behave in it and toward it.

WHAT'S THIS... WHO DAT?!

TRUST IN THE LORD WITH ALL YOUR HEART AND LEAN NOT TO YOUR OWN UNDERSTANDING; IN ALL YOUR WAYS ACKNOWLEDGE HIM, AND HE WILL DIRECT YOUR PATH.

PROVERBS 3:5-7

Our own understanding is limited to what we can see, and here's the truth: we can't see enough to know enough. Our understanding is incomplete, and it always will be. When we lean on our own interpretation, we mislabel things because we don't have the full picture. We assign names to seasons we don't understand. We create definitions in the dark.

And the problem with creating definitions in the dark is that you can only define based on what you think you see. The disciples thought they saw a ghost, but it was Jesus. You think you see punishment, but it's preparation. You think you see nothing, but there's actually something. Your eyes can trick you, and your imagination will fill in the blanks with fear.

That's why God never asked us to lean on understanding. He asked us to lean on Him. Because while your vision is blocked by the night, His sight isn't limited by darkness. He sees what you cannot, and He knows what you do not.

Mislabeling is dangerous. Because when you call it wrong, you live it wrong. And when you live it wrong, you miss the grace, the growth, and the God who's been with you the whole time.

Sometimes God shows up in ways you don't recognize, and fear will always misinterpret Him. If you're not careful, you'll treat your miracle like a monster.

CAN YOU SEE IT NOW

One of the biggest misconceptions we carry about life is that we need clarity for the future. We pray for light at the end of the tunnel, asking God to show us how things will work out, where this season is leading, and what's next. But that's not what Genesis shows us. From the very beginning, God reveals a principle: you don't need clarity for where you're going—you need clarity for where you are.

Genesis opens with the words, "In the beginning God created the heavens and the earth." Notice the tense—created. Past tense. It was already finished. But here's the thing: God gives us no detail about Heaven in that moment. None. Because it wasn't relevant to us yet. What He does give us is detail about the Earth—because that's where we are. And clarity is only ever required for where you are, not where you're going.

That revelation right there cuts deep, because most of our anxiety comes from trying to understand the destination before we've even gotten a handle on the present. We get stuck, lost, and overwhelmed not because the future is unclear, but because we've ignored the darkness in our now.

Genesis says the earth was formless, empty, and dark.

Formless (Tohuw): without structure, chaotic, lying in waste. Full of potential, but purposeless.

Empty (Bohuw): vacant, uninhabited. Like a shopping mall with the lights on but no one inside.

Dark (Choshek): obscure, difficult to understand, hidden.

That's the picture of what life feels like sometimes—no clear shape, no sense of purpose, no understanding of what's happening around you. That's when we throw up our hands and say, "I don't see nothing."

But here's the problem: calling it "nothing" is a mislabel. And we already know—whatever you mislabel, you will mismanage.

The text says, "And the Spirit of God was hovering over the waters." Wait—waters? Where did those come from? Even in the formless, empty, dark void, there was something there. God's Spirit was moving, brooding, fluttering over it.

Here's the hard truth: we often treat what we don't understand as if it's nothing. But "nothing" is a lie. Nothingness isn't the absence of God—it's the absence of recognition.

That's why God has a problem with "nothing." Because "nothing" is what you confess when you've failed to steward what He's already given you. To say you have "nothing" is to suggest, "God, You didn't give me enough." And that is never the truth.

Bishop T.D. Jakes says it best: "God doesn't make tables and chairs. He makes trees." God gives you raw material, and then He tells you, "Create." But because it doesn't look like the finished product, we call it "nothing." We pray for a table and get frustrated when He gives us a forest. We ask for a chair and get mad when He hands us a tree trunk. The issue is not the absence of provision—it's the absence of perception.

And that's why your darkness needs illumination. Revelation is the only thing that turns "I don't see nothing" into "I see something." Light doesn't change what's there—it simply reveals it.

The very first thing God created wasn't land, or plants, or animals. It was light. Illumination. Awareness. Insight. Because nothing else can be formed, filled, or purposed until there is revelation. Light makes sense of the mess. Light separates what is useful from what is waste. Light brings identity, and what's recognizable can finally be used.

And Jesus echoed this when He said, "I am the Light of the world." He wasn't speaking poetically—He was laying down a blueprint. Work while it's day, He said, because night brings confusion. Weeping may endure for a night, but joy shows up with clarity. And here's the kicker: a new day doesn't start when the clock strikes midnight. A new day starts when light breaks in. Illumination is what signals the shift, not the numbers on the clock.

I've lived this. I went through one of the darkest seasons of my life—losing my job, my place, my car, my sense of stability. Depression had me in its grip. Suicidal thoughts clouded my mind. On my birthday, I stayed in bed all day, crying, feeling like my life had collapsed. And in that night season, I tried to find comfort in Scripture and ended up in Ecclesiastes 1 and 2. Bad move. Those are the "everything is meaningless" chapters, and when you're already depressed, that's not the encouragement you need.

But then I got to chapter 3, verse 11: "He has made everything beautiful in its time." That verse hit me like a beam of light piercing the darkness. It told me: yes, this is ugly right now, but it's ugly on purpose. And when the time comes, it will be beautiful. Not because I made it so, but because God already spoke beauty over it.

That was illumination. That was revelation. That was God whispering to me in the dark, "This is not nothing. This is raw. This is process. But if you'll trust Me, you'll see the beauty in time."

So what's a good day? A good day isn't when everything is perfect. A good day is when what was formless gains structure. When what was confusing gains clarity. When what was dark gets illuminated. A good day is when you stop calling your tree "nothing" and start building your table.

WHAT'S THIS... WHO DAT?!

THE WINK SAYS IT ALL

When I was a kid, I loved Barney. Big purple dinosaur, singing "I love you, you love me," carrying all the joy in the world. But what always stuck with me wasn't just the songs or the lessons—it was the very end of each episode. When Barney went back to doll form, right before the credits rolled, the camera would pan in close. And just before the screen faded out, his eye would blink in a way that looked like a wink. It was small, quick, almost unnoticeable if you weren't looking for it. But to a kid like me, it felt personal. Like Barney was saying, "Hey, I see you. Thanks for being here. We'll do it again soon."

That's the image that comes to mind when I think about God's presence in the middle of life's storms.

Here's what I love about God: He doesn't always shout. Sometimes He winks.

Think about Genesis. The earth was formless, empty, and dark. Chaos. Vacancy. Obscurity. And into all that confusion, God leaned forward and whispered, "Let there be light." That was His wink. Not a full explanation, not a 10-step strategy, not a map of the future—just illumination. Just enough for us to see that there was already something there.

And that's the power of a wink. A wink is quick. Subtle. Easy to miss if you're not paying attention. And that's what makes it so personal. A wink says, "I see you." A wink says, "I'm with you, even if I don't spell it out." A wink is confidence without over-explaining.

That's exactly what Jesus did on the water in Matthew 14. The disciples were terrified in the storm. They looked out into the darkness and saw a figure on the waves. Their imagination filled in the gaps and fear took over. "It's a ghost!" they cried. But Jesus didn't preach a sermon in that moment. He didn't calm the storm first to prove a point. He simply winked with His words: "Take courage. It is I. Don't be afraid." Just enough revelation for them to know it was Him.

And He's still doing that for us.

Jesus has a way of winking at you in the middle of your worst night. Sometimes it's a Scripture that hits your chest when you weren't even looking for it. Sometimes it's a phone call from a friend at the exact moment you were ready to give up. Sometimes it's a lyric in a song that feels like it was written for you. Sometimes it's a random check in the mail when you're out of options. That's not coincidence—that's a wink.

But here's the thing about a wink: you have to look up to catch it. If your eyes are buried in despair, buried in fear, buried in the assumption that nothing good can come out of this season, you'll miss it. You'll keep calling Him a ghost. You'll keep running from your help. You'll mislabel the wink as something else.

The wink is God's way of saying, "Don't lean on your own understanding. You can't see enough to know enough. But if you'll just catch My wink, you'll know I'm here."

It's like seeing someone across a crowded room. They don't have to shout your name. They don't have to fight their way to the front. All it takes is a wink, and you know you've been seen. That wink cuts through the noise, through the crowd, through the chaos. And that's what Jesus does in your storm. He doesn't always calm it right away. Sometimes He just winks, because His presence is the peace.

So let me leave you with this: God has been winking at you all along. In Genesis, it was light. In the Gospels, it was Jesus. In your life, it may be the small, subtle moments that don't make sense until later—until you realize, "Oh, that was Him the whole time."

The Divine Wink is reassurance that even when you don't see clearly, He does. Even when you don't understand, He's near. Even when you think it's nothing, He shows you there's always something.

    The challenge is: will you notice it? Will you pause long enough to catch it? Because the wink is subtle. And if you're too distracted by the dark, you'll miss the Light staring you right in the face.

"WHY WOULD YOU KEEP LETTING STUFF HAPPEN TO ME? DON'T YOU SEE THAT I'M TRYING? WHAT'S THE FREAKING POINT?!?!"

HEY GOD,
WHY ALLOW THIS?

Today, I just really feel like giving up...
on You, on life, on everything.
Why does my life have to be this hard?
Why does everything keep happening back to back?
Are You trying to make me quit? Do You actually want me to break? Because right now—I don't have any more fight left.
Why does bad stuff keep happening to me?
I know I'm not perfect, but I try to live right. And yet here I am—frustrated at You, God. What do You even do with all the power You have?
It's already hard enough being a Black man in America. Every time a cop car gets behind me, my heart sinks into my lap. But to actually get pulled over? LEAVING church at that? At this point, I'm mad. Because if I had just stayed home, I wouldn't have even been in that situation. Is this my reward for being faithful? A cop pulling me over, calling for backup, throwing my stuff out of my car, searching for drugs I don't have, after I told them over and over I don't do that.

my cell phone's off Because of my financial situation.
I couldn't even call anybody.
What if something happened to me?
It would have been their word against mine.
Do You see the climate?
Weapons?!
God, I wear Toy Story Crocs.
I was leaving church. I didn't look aggressive.
Yet there I was—sitting on the curb, watching them tow my car. All because when I stopped at the red light, my front tire was on the crosswalk. You know the situation I'm in.
Why didn't You shield me from that?
I'm at my breaking point.
How am I supposed to get my car from the impound when the balance keeps going up every day?
I can't even take care of my phone bill right now.
God, what is all this about?
I'm trying to stay strong. I'm trying to keep the faith.
But why do the cards never fall in my favor?
I'm not a quitter—and You know that.
But today...
I feel like throwing in the towel and quitting everything.
I can't do this anymore.

6.
TAKEN

Grief is its own kind of storm. It doesn't just pass through — it lingers, it shifts, and it blindsides you when you least expect it.

July 25, 2022, is a day I can't get out of my head. It lives in my body, in my memory, in my bones. It replays when I don't want it to, and no matter how much I try, I can't release it. That day didn't just change me—it ruined me.

I remember walking into my grandmother's hospice room around 12:30 in the afternoon. The air was heavy, like it already knew something I didn't want to admit. It was just me and my aunt in the room, and I grabbed a chair to sit next to her. As soon as I looked at her, I knew the end was near. Her feet were cold. Her catheter bag was empty, meaning her body had stopped producing urine. She was nonverbal, not eating, slipping in and out of consciousness. Even as I write this, I feel the sharp puncture of memory in my chest. This was not the Granny I was used to seeing. Her eyes were roaming, unfocused. Her mouth hung open and twisted in a way that made me want to cry and scream at the same time. I wanted her back, but deep down, I'm a realist—and I knew she wasn't coming back.

Still, I reached for her hand. "Hey Granny... it's Grandpa," I whispered, calling myself what she always called me. "I'm here... I'll hold your hand like you used to hold mine." And something happened. Something holy. With what little strength she had left, she turned her head toward me and started mouthing words. I could see the fight in her face, see the frustration when no sound came out. I tried to calm her, but then in an instant, her body began convulsing. I was holding her hand, helpless, begging her not to try so hard—when all of a sudden, she stopped breathing.

Shock gripped me. My body went cold. "Girl, I know you lying," I shouted through my tears, "don't do this to me." And just like that, as if she heard me, breath came back into her body.

The thought that my grandmother could take her last breath while I was holding her hand shook me to my core. But it didn't just happen once. Every hour on the hour, the same thing repeated. I held my grandmother's hand seven different times thinking it was her last breath. Seven times I thought she was gone, and seven times I was wrong. By the time the rest of my family rolled in, we all were on edge. I became the lookout. From across the room, I would warn, "Somebody grab her hand—it's about to happen again." And eventually, it did. At 12:10 AM, the final breath left her body. This time, it didn't return.

The funeral came and went like a blur. Family gathered, food was made, people checked in. But then, as always, everyone went home. The phone calls stopped. The food stopped showing up. And the silence started to speak. The memories wouldn't leave me alone. Something as small as seeing a bag of Bugle chips at the store would jolt me back into that hospice room.

One day, I stopped by my aunt's house, who lived around the corner from my grandmother's, but before I got there, I decided to drive past Granny's one last time. I wasn't ready for what I saw. My grandmother always had a little license plate, that read JESUS, sitting in the front window by the door. I can't explain it, but as I walked up, I half expected to hear her voice say, "Hold on Grandpa, I'm coming to open the door." Instead, I peered through the window and saw the unthinkable—her entire house was empty. Cleared out. Stripped. Everything gone, like she had never lived there at all. That house that once smelled like cornbread, laughter, and love was being prepped for someone else. And in that moment, it hit me—she was really gone. Not just physically. Not just her body. But her presence. Her essence. Her everything. And with that realization, I felt like a huge chunk of my heart had been taken.

That harsh reality sank me deeper into depression. Each day it became harder to get out of bed. Harder to breathe. Harder to exist. My FMLA time off was running out, so I tried going back to work. But the grief was like a wave crashing over me. I sat at my desk, tears falling, unable to do anything. My HR director took one look at me and extended my leave. They knew I wasn't ready. Truthfully, I don't think anyone knew just how not ready I was.

Because the world expected me to return to "normal Josh." The Josh who made people comfortable. The Josh who could laugh and lighten a room. But that version of me had died in that hospice room. Didn't anyone realize what had been taken from me? Grief doesn't just hurt—it cripples you. I didn't have anything to laugh about anymore. I withdrew from people, isolating myself so I wouldn't bring others down. My tolerance grew thin. My anger grew quick. And deep down, I was scared. I had always wanted children, but after this, the thought of one day losing them terrified me. If grief was the price of love, I didn't want to love anymore. Because love was too expensive.

I thought I was strong enough. I thought I had already processed it. But then the waves kept coming, one after another, and the storm refused to end.

Each day got worse. Waking up felt like punishment. I started resenting God for keeping me alive. It's strange to feel grateful and angry in the same breath. To thank Him for breath in your lungs while simultaneously wishing He would take it away. I used to love natural light—sunlight always felt like God's smile. But during this season, the dark felt safer. Darkness wrapped itself around me like a blanket, hiding me from the pain daylight revealed.

I didn't want to live anymore. People kept asking, "How are you doing?" and I never knew what to say. I wasn't stable enough to give an honest answer, and I was too tired to fake one. The grief was unbearable. I even started planning my death. I took the spare key to my apartment and slid it under the trash bin by the front door. My logic was simple: when I didn't wake up, one of my friends—knowing how they are—would eventually stop by. They'd find me, and at least I'd get buried properly.

I'll never forget the day I finally dragged myself out of bed after days of not showering. I ran a hot bath, filled the tub to the brim, and climbed in. I hit play on Kirk Franklin's Help Me Believe and let it play on repeat. Sitting in that water, with tears streaming down my face, I cried out, "God, if this is not going to get better, will you please just take me?" And I meant it. I wasn't being dramatic. I wasn't being religious. I was begging.

I felt like I was drowning in grief, so the thought of actually drowning no longer felt like torture—it felt like relief. My heart was beyond broken. My will to live was gone. Hope wasn't just lost; it felt stolen. Taken. The future seemed like a cruel joke, and the only thing I could look forward to was death. Waking up to a world where what was no longer is—that reality is unbearable. And I don't care how saved you are, how many scriptures you quote, how many tongues you speak in—grief like that will shake the very foundation of your faith.

In the thick of my grief, I did nothing but binge television shows and rewatch some of my favorite movies. It wasn't just to pass time—it was survival. The silence was too loud, the weight of my thoughts too heavy, so I drowned them out with the comfort of stories. I've always been in love with good stories. Beyond entertainment, stories carry something deeper. They have value. They mirror us back to ourselves. They help us make sense of things we can't put words to. Stories have this strange, sacred power: they can make you feel seen, they can unlock something you didn't even know was hidden, and sometimes they can change your life altogether.

During this season, one show in particular gripped me—Netflix's The Sandman. I had heard the hype, but from the very first episode, I knew this wasn't just good television—it was smart, layered writing that reached into places I didn't expect. It was myth and metaphor colliding. I was hooked from the beginning until the very end. But there was one scene, tucked away in episode four of the first season, that seared itself into my soul. The episode was titled A Hope in Hell. And honestly, that title alone felt like my autobiography at the time. Because that's exactly what life felt like—hell without hope.

In that episode, Dream (Morpheus) journeys into Hell to retrieve his stolen helm. He finds the demon who possesses it, but reclaiming it isn't as simple as reaching out and taking it back. He has to fight for it. Yet the fight isn't one of fists or swords—it's one of words. Specifically, "I am" statements. Whatever Dream or his opponent claimed to be determined their method of attack, and the stronger declaration trumped the weaker one.

At first, the battle is imaginative but almost playful: Dream and his opponent morph into animals, wolves devouring, serpents striking, birds swooping. But as the fight progresses, so does the weight of the words. The deeper the "I am," the more devastating the attack. Dream finds himself against Lucifer herself, who steps in to battle on behalf of the demon. And from the beginning, it is clear—she is stronger, sharper, more cunning. Round after round, Dream is crushed, left weaker, breathless, nearly undone. Finally, Lucifer towers over him, sneering, and declares with chilling triumph: "I am anti-life. The darkness at the end of everything."

That line pierced me because it felt like my reality. Grief felt like anti-life. Depression felt like darkness at the end of everything. I knew what it was to be on the floor, gasping for breath while life seemed to mock me. I could see myself in Dream's posture—flattened, weary, at the mercy of an enemy I couldn't overcome. Lucifer's taunt, her question—what could survive anti-life?—echoed in my own spirit. What could survive this pain? What could outlast this grief?

And then it happened. Dream, lying there, voice faint and broken, whispered two words that turned the entire fight: "I am Hope." And everything changed. The power shifted. Lucifer's sinister grin collapsed into a look of defeat, and Dream rose again. The battle was over—not because he had more brute strength, but because he had something stronger than despair. He had hope.

That scene undid me. It was as if God reached through a fantasy series and tapped me on the shoulder, reminding me of something I had forgotten: hope has resurrection power. Hope has the ability to raise you from the ashes, to lift you off the floor, to breathe life back into places you thought were gone forever. Hopelessness, on the other hand, is an assassin. It doesn't just steal your energy—it convinces you that there's no reason to get up, no reason to try again, no reason to live. Without hope, life itself becomes fleeting.

And in that moment, sitting in my apartment with the screen still glowing, I realized something I hadn't been able to name before. My fight to get out of bed every morning wasn't just about losing my grandmother. Along with my grandmother, I had lost my hope. And without hope, I wasn't sure I wanted to keep living.

That's when I had to redefine it for myself. What is hope, really? It's not just optimism, not just a vague wish for things to get better. Biblically, hope is expectation—something to look forward to. A future you can lean your weight on. Hope is the picture of that tomorrow. Hope is a lifeline. Hope is a platform to stand on when everything else is sinking.

TAKEN

HOPE DEFERRED MAKES THE HEART SICK...
PROVERBS 13:12(NIV)

I grasped the notion that my hope was depleted, but even with that awareness, I had no will to do anything about it. I wasn't ready to fight back, wasn't ready to pray hard prayers or even try to "push through." Instead of getting up to pursue hope, I went on a far less noble quest: finding my next binge watch. That's where I was in life—grief-stricken, heartbroken, and leaning on the numbing power of television. I didn't expect God to meet me in that space, and certainly not through the "Continue Watching" section of Netflix or Disney+. But that's the thing about God: He doesn't wait until you're in a sanctuary or on your knees with oil on your forehead. Sometimes He shows up in your scrolling, sliding you a recommendation you never knew you needed. And in my case, He suggested Finding Nemo.

Now, to know me is to know that I am a die-hard Disney Pixar fan. In my humble opinion, they produced the greatest animated film of all time—Toy Story. Argue with yourself if you must, but Toy Story paved the way and still stands relevant today. So when the Lord didn't suggest Toy Story but instead nudged me toward Finding Nemo, I rolled my eyes a little. Don't get me wrong, I love Finding Nemo—it's a classic—but I wasn't in the mood for that particular film. It felt too lighthearted for the darkness I was in. Yet, the nudges from the Holy Spirit grew stronger until I finally gave in.

I have a running joke about Disney Pixar: somebody in that studio has the purest form of the Holy Ghost. I'm convinced of it. Because the way these films slip into ministry, the way they sneak past your defenses and end up preaching to you—it ought to be studied. Who knew that my deliverance, my lifeline, would come through a movie about clownfish? But I've learned that when God recommends something, He's not sending you in blind. He always gives you a preview. So before pressing play on the full movie, I pulled up the trailer on YouTube.

That preview set me up. Watching it, you'd walk away thinking Finding Nemo is just a heartwarming story about a father's adventurous quest across the ocean to find his lost little boy. The trailer makes it sound like Nemo simply wandered off, like he just got lost somewhere in the big blue sea. Cute, right? But the reality was far from cute. Nemo wasn't lost—he was taken. And that distinction makes all the difference.

The movie opens by introducing us to Marlin and Coral, a clownfish couple freshly moved into their dream home. It's beautiful, a perfect place for the family they are about to have. The camera pans across the reef to show us over four hundred eggs waiting to hatch. Marlin is brimming with pride. He's secure, excited, ready to build a future. The neighborhood is nice, the schools are better, the environment feels safe. Everything is as it should be. And then, in a single moment, everything changes. A predator sweeps in and devours all of Coral and the eggs in one horrifying strike. Just like that, his entire world is stripped away.

That scene broke me wide open because it mirrored what grief had done in my own life. Transition happens without announcement. Loss doesn't call ahead to schedule a convenient time. It barges in and rearranges everything you thought was stable. Watching Marlin's devastation triggered the ache of my own. It reminded me of how fast I lost my grandmother. How quickly one day could undo all the days before it.

I almost turned the movie off right there. I couldn't take it. But before I could reach for the remote, I felt God whisper to me: "Look, Josh. I know you feel like you've lost everything, but look again. You lost a lot, but you did not lose it all." And at that exact moment on the screen, Marlin peers over the empty nest of eggs. The hole is barren, evidence of devastation. But nestled there, small and fragile, is one egg left behind. In the midst of overwhelming loss, Marlin realizes something survived. One remained.

That's when the Holy Spirit pressed in harder: "I know you want to, but you cannot die here. Cry over what's gone, but don't forsake what you still have left. Wake up and strengthen what remains." I sat there, tears in my eyes, realizing that while my grief was valid, my story wasn't over. I had to tend to what was left.

I had watched Finding Nemo hundreds of times before, but this time it hit different. For the first time, I understood why Marlin was so protective over Nemo. He wasn't just parenting a child; he was guarding his last remaining piece of hope. When you've lost almost everything, the fear of losing what remains becomes suffocating. You hold tighter. You guard harder. You love with a desperate kind of intensity because you simply cannot afford to lose again. If you do, you're afraid you'll lose your mind right along with it.

That's when I realized: Nemo wasn't just Marlin's son. Nemo was his last sliver of hope. He became the reason Marlin got up every morning. The reason he kept swimming. The reason he kept breathing. When you've lost nearly everything, hope becomes your oxygen, and losing it feels like suffocation.

The story moves on—Nemo, of course, is captured by a diver and taken away. And in that moment, Marlin's greatest fear comes to pass. The very thing that kept him alive is snatched from him. His last piece of hope is taken.

And here's the question that gripped me so tightly I couldn't escape it: What do you do when your last bit of hope gets taken?

Most of us, if we're honest, want to give up right there. To wave the white flag and stop fighting. To quit before life can snatch anything else. But as I sat there with God holding my heart together through a children's movie, I felt Him take my hand and whisper: "You simply can't."

BUT JESUS IMMEDIATELY SAID TO THEM: "TAKE COURAGE! IT IS I. DON'T BE AFRAID."
MATTHEW 14:27 (NIV)

By now in Matthew 14, we're stationed at verse 27. The disciples are still in the middle of that storm—hours of battling wind and waves that don't seem to relent. Their boat is being tossed back and forth, the rain pounding, the waters raging. It's one thing to go through a storm that hits quickly and passes quickly. You can breathe easier after those. But this one? This one is dragging on and on, and exhaustion has set in. The fight to stay afloat is one thing, but the fight to keep believing you'll actually survive it is another battle altogether.

And if the storm wasn't enough, now there's something unfamiliar coming toward them on the water. They can't quite make it out through the haze and the rain, so fear fills the vacuum of their understanding. By this point, hopelessness has settled in, just like it had in me as I laid in my bed surrounded by darkness, tormented by grief. Hopelessness doesn't just sit quietly in the corner—it takes over the whole room. It becomes the elephant that demands attention, pressing questions into your spirit: Is anyone coming for me? Can anyone really help me? Will this ever change? Or is this how my story ends?

And then, Jesus steps into the scene. He walks on the very waves that are threatening to sink them. He comes near enough for His voice to be heard over the storm. And He doesn't just announce His presence—He makes a demand: "Take courage. It is I. Don't be afraid."

That line stopped me in my tracks. I had to scratch my bald head and ask: why did He say take courage and not have courage? On the surface, those two words feel interchangeable. But they're not. "Have" suggests ownership, possession, something sitting in your hands. "Take," however, is active. It requires reaching, grasping, pulling something close, doing something with it. "Take" implies motion.

It reminded me of something I learned back in school about potential and kinetic energy. Potential energy is stored energy—power that exists by virtue of position or possibility. In plain terms, it's energy that could be released but isn't being used yet. Some of us live there. We have all the ideas, all the dreams, all the strategies, all the talents—but we never move. It's potential stacked high in our closets and notebooks but never converted into action.

Kinetic energy, on the other hand, is energy in motion. It's the work needed to accelerate something from rest to velocity. It's the push, the step, the swing, the choice to move. Once a body gains kinetic energy, it holds it unless something slows it down. And here's the revelation: to "have" courage is potential energy. To "take" courage is kinetic energy. Having it doesn't help you if you never use it. You can be gifted, talented, anointed, creative, prophetic—and still defeated if you never put it into motion.

Why don't we move? Fear. That's the real culprit. Fear freezes potential and paralyzes destiny. Fear convinces you that sitting still is safer, even when it's actually suffocating you. Jesus said in John 8:32, "You shall know the truth, and the truth shall make you free." Truth unlocks movement. So if truth is freedom, lies are bondage. And many of us are enslaved not because God hasn't given us courage, but because we've swallowed lies that keep us from taking it.

I know this all too well. Typically, I can knock out a book in thirty days. But this book you're holding? It took a full year. Because when my grandmother died, fear imprisoned my creativity. Since I was a child, I've loved to write. Stories, plays, films, books—I lived with a pen in my hand. My last book before this one was published in 2020. I planned to finish my Sins of a Mother series right after because those fans are relentless. They want the ending, and they want it now. I even started mapping it out in 2021. Notes upon notes filled my phone with character arcs and loose threads.

And then came Mary Ann. That character was loosely based on my grandmother. While shopping at Walmart one day, her storyline hit me in a wave, and I rushed to my Notes app to jot it all down. The details I wrote ended up unfolding in real life the very next year. My grandmother's reality mirrored my fiction. That shook me. It terrified me. I felt like I had written her death into existence. And in that guilt and fear, I put my pen down. I boxed up my creativity. I locked it away like it was dangerous. I told myself I was done.

For five years, I didn't write. Five years, I withheld what God had placed in me. Five years, I suffocated my own air because I was afraid of the weight of my responsibility. And here's the hard truth I had to face: while my heart was broken and my grief was real, I was disobeying God. He gave us all the same command in Genesis: "Be fruitful and multiply." That doesn't just mean children—it means produce, expand, create, multiply what He's given you. Grief is a reason to pause, yes. But it cannot be your excuse to stop. God is still expecting a return on His investment.

The parable of the talents makes it plain: even the servant with the least was still expected to produce something. To bury what you've been given is to rob the world of what it needs and to rob God of His glory. The people connected to your gift go malnourished when you shut down. My ability to write never left me. I never lost my potential. What I lost was my motion. And without motion, there is no momentum.

That's why Jesus said, "Take courage." He knew the disciples had it in them—they just hadn't activated it yet. He didn't want the lie of destruction to immobilize them. He wanted them to grab hold of what was already theirs and put it in motion. And you're reading this book today because I did exactly that. I didn't just have courage—I took it. I put it into action. That doesn't mean the fear evaporated. It means I refused to let fear keep me stuck. I did it anyway.

Courage is not the absence of fear—it is obedience in the face of it. Courage says, "I'm scared, but I'll move." Courage says, "I don't know the outcome, but I'll step." Courage is strength in the face of pain and grief. Nobody has to understand your courage. It's not for them—it's for your destiny.

It takes courage to get out of your head. To get out of your trauma. To get out of your PTSD. To get out of your stress. To get out of your reasoning. To get out of your own way. And every time you choose courage, you convert potential into kinetic. You create momentum.

Marlin in Finding Nemo understood this. He could have stopped. And truth be told, he wanted to stop many times. But he kept moving because his hope was at stake. Along the way, he met Dory. Now, everybody jokes that Dory had short-term memory loss. But watching it this time, I realized she carried a spiritual gift: she embodied Philippians 3. Paul said, "I haven't attained it yet. I don't have all the answers. But this one thing I do—I forget what's behind me, and I press forward toward the goal." That was Dory. She may not have remembered everything, but she remembered how to press forward.

One of the most iconic lines in the film comes when Marlin is frustrated, tired, and ready to quit. Dory looks at him and says, "When life gets you down, you know what you gotta do? Just keep swimming." That line isn't just cute—it's prophetic. It's the mantra of courage.

I know what it is to get tired of waking up and seeing the empty seat at the table. I know what it is to be brokenhearted, to face reminders of what you've lost every single day. But hear me: you cannot stop here. Cry if you need to. Grieve if you must. But keep pressing. Just keep swimming.

And right here, I shift. Because this is bigger than me. In the name of Jesus, I declare life over you. Life to the full. We come against every spirit of death—whether willful or premature. The blood of Jesus is against you. Depression, hopelessness, anxiety, defeat, weariness, quitting, fear—the blood is against you. We cancel every death contract our mouths signed out of grief. We speak a new language now, and it is life. We shall not die, but we shall live and declare the works of the Lord.

Don't lose your motion. Don't let fear freeze your potential. Just keep swimming.

Because here's the secret: courage without fear isn't courage—it's comfort. Real courage acknowledges the storm, faces the waves, and still steps out on the water anyway. Jesus said, "Take courage. It is I. Don't be afraid." Anchor yourself in His presence, remember what He said, and keep moving forward.

Even Dory knew it: the light you find along the way matters. At one point, when things looked dark and hopeless, it was the light that revealed the address—P. Sherman, 42 Wallaby Way, Sydney. The Word of God works the same way. "Thy word is a lamp unto my feet and a light unto my path." You need people like Dory who will help you remember what God has already spoken, even when you forget everything else.

So I say to you, the journey may be long, the waves may be rough, and the storm may feel unending. But don't stop. Don't give up. Go back and remember what God showed you. He promised restoration. He promised hope. And hope and life are about to reunite in your story.

Don't stop believing. Don't stop pressing. Because after it's all said and done, He who promised will come, and He will not delay. It may tarry, but wait for it. Hope is not lost. Courage is not absent. You just have to take it.

TAKEN

Yes—grief took something from you. It robbed you of the person you loved, the stability you depended on, the life you once knew. It left an empty seat at the table, a silence in the room, and a hollow space in your heart that words can't fully describe. Grief has a way of reaching into your chest and snatching away pieces of you that you didn't even realize were vulnerable. It shifts your world in ways that feel unfair, abrupt, and irreversible. I won't pretend it didn't take something. It did. And if you're honest, it may feel like it took everything.

But hear me: hopelessness is not the end of your story. Hopelessness is loud, but it is not final. It whispers lies that nothing will ever change, that you'll never recover, that life as you knew it is over and so is your reason to live. But courage—the kind you reach for, the kind you take—is how you reclaim what was stolen. Courage doesn't erase what happened, but it transforms what remains. Courage says, "I will not let this storm dictate my destination. I will not let this pain become my prison." Courage is the key that unlocks motion when grief has you paralyzed.

So here is my charge to you: Take courage. Don't just acknowledge that it exists—grab it, own it, walk with it, use it. Take courage when fear tells you to freeze. Take courage when hopelessness tries to convince you there's nothing left. Take courage when your heart screams to stop, but your spirit knows you need to keep pressing.

And when you take courage, make a decision in your heart that you will not come back empty. Too many of us bury our gifts, bury our voices, bury our callings because of the weight of loss. But hear me clearly: your hurt is real, but it cannot be the reason you stop. You may pause, but you cannot quit. Don't come back to God empty-handed when He has placed treasures in you meant to feed nations. Don't let grief silence the gift that somebody else's survival is depending on. What you have left is still valuable. What you have left still matters.

So yes, you've been taken through loss, through grief, through hopelessness. But you are not defeated. Lift your head. Wipe your tears. Grab hold of courage and step forward. Strengthen what remains. Keep swimming. And above all—live. Live so fully, so faithfully, that your life itself becomes the proof that grief does not get the last word.

Yes, grief took something from you. But hopelessness isn't the end of your story. Courage is how you reclaim what was stolen — and courage is what Jesus is handing you right now.

"YOU KNOW WHAT?! I'M SO TIRED OF HAVE LIVE OUT EXPERIENCES FOR OTHER PEOPLE... WHAT ABOUT ME?! DO I MATTER AT ALL? I'M HELP TO ALL THESE PEOPLE, WHO'S GONNA HELP ME?"

HEY GOD,
WHY'D YOU WIRE ME LIKE THIS?!

God, I'm really starting to feel like You're setting me up.
Why in the world would You make me this analytical—
and then tell me to do outrageous stuff?
Do You not see how mentally exhausted I am?
DO YOU HATE ME?!
Most days I don't know if I'm coming or going.
"Have faith," they said.
But what happens when I believe You—over and over
again—and it still seems like it doesn't work?
I don't want to hate You...
but You're not making it easy for me.
I've given my life to You, for You to use—
and it feels like it counts for nothing.
My mind spins from sun up to sun down.
Always analyzing. Always trying to figure it out.
Why can't I just embrace seasons where I can simply
show up?
Then people say I look angry and frustrated all the time.
I AM.
Because my brain needs a break...but life won't give me
one.

Why do You make it so hard to know if it's really You or not?
I'm trying to do Your will but it's not clear.
I'm trying to be in the right place, in position—
but then You take Your time giving direction and instruction.
None of this feels fair.
DO YOU WANT ME TO FAIL?!
Nothing in my life makes sense right now.
You tell me not to worry, not to stress—but how?
Am I just supposed to "go with the flow"?
Do You know I'm starting to have panic attacks now?
I'm not as strong as I used to be.
It's hitting me differently this time.
I can't control my mind—
and now my body is attacking itself as a result.
What kind of life is that?
I didn't ask for this.
You wired me to think deeply—
so why does it feel like You strapped a bomb to my back and it's about to detonate?
UGH. I'm so frustrated with You.
You keep telling me to do things that don't make sense.
WHY?!

7.
BLESSED *RE*•ASSURANCE

Faith is messy. It's not the polished Sunday-morning version with the right words and perfect posture. Real faith limps, wrestles, and sometimes looks more like survival than triumph.

If nothing else, I am a realist. I never liked probability or hypotheticals. Give me the real. One of my strong suits, as my therapist pointed out, is my level of awareness and assessment. I am an aware king. I don't walk around lying to myself or sugarcoating my own truth. Even when it's ugly and even when the truth doesn't flatter me, I face it head-on. Every year at the close of December, I get still. I quiet myself, sit with myself, and I take inventory. I pull out my mental pen and pad and I list my stats for the year—my wins, my losses, the things I accomplished, and the things I fumbled. I jot down what people have said about me—whether it was whispered, implied, or said directly. Then I sit with what I know to be true about myself. And here's the thing: I don't give myself a pass. I know that when my life feels out of control, I can lean toward erratic behaviors. That doesn't make it right, but it does mean I'm aware of it. Nobody has to pull me to the side and tell me about me. Nine times out of ten, I already know. Growth is something I measure because awareness is the only way I can evolve.

And in all my self-awareness, there are two things I know without a shadow of doubt. The first is this: I'm not a hustler.

Now, don't get it twisted—I grew up in Oak Cliff. If you know, you know. Oak Cliff is hustler central. Everybody out there is trying to flip something, sell something, push something, get to the money. Hustling is the way of the land.

But somehow, that gene skipped right over me. I'm not wired like that. I've never subscribed to hustle-and-grind culture. I don't wake up every morning thinking about how I can "secure the bag." My philosophy has always been simple: what's mine is mine, and if it's truly mine, then it doesn't have to run away from me. Why am I chasing what God already assigned to my life? If I'm in the right place, holding the right posture, then what's mine is going to come find me.

That's why I don't dabble in marketing or sales. The quickest job I ever quit was a vendor job where they stationed me inside Sam's Club to sell cable. Oh baby, listen—I went to lunch and never came back. I was so over it that they literally had to call and beg me to come pick up my first check. Honestly, they could've kept it. After taxes, it came out to $5.68. To me, that was not money; that was disrespect.

Now, one of my sisters? She's a hustler for real—in the best sense of the word. She was the first one to land a job at sixteen. McDonald's. She hated it, but she kept showing up because she liked having her own money. Meanwhile, my mama kept looking at me like, "So what you gone do?" But here's the thing: I've never been lazy. I just refuse to settle. I'm not chasing checks that come with chaos attached. My sister would come home smelling like fry grease, working crazy shifts, and dealing with all kinds of stress. I knew then and there, that wasn't for me.

So, at eighteen, when I did step into the workforce, I went straight into corporate America. No flipping burgers, no waving signs on the corner. I went where I knew my brain could thrive. I landed a job as a Compliance Researcher, sitting at a desk with a title and weekends off. Let's be clear, the interview wasn't just about credentials. It was a mixture of charm and intelligence—my cute way of saying I knew my stuff, but I also flirted my way in. There I was, eighteen years old, making $15.50 an hour while my sister was clocking in for minimum wage. The math was mathing, and that was my kind of carrying.

The second thing I know about myself is this: I am not a risk taker. Oh God, no. Impulsiveness is not in my DNA. I'm way too analytical for that. Now, calculated risks? Sure. But those folks who just up and quit their jobs with nothing lined up, move to a new city with $500 in their pocket, and somehow figure it out—I envy them. If I ever tried that, I'd probably end up in a psych ward. That's why, even though I got accepted into an acting school in Los Angeles, I didn't go. The cost of living was sky high, I'm an incredibly picky eater, and I knew struggle-life and I weren't going to get along. I need footing. I need a sense of ground beneath me.

That's even true in relationships. I don't take risks there either. I've got trauma attached to that, but the truth is still the truth. I don't shoot my shot. I'll flirt, but only once I know the other person is flirting back. As a kid, I'd go to the movies or the skating rink with my cousins, and they'd be hollering at girls left and right, coming home with phone numbers like trophies. Me? My paper stayed blank. The only real risks I take are on stage or in front of a camera—and even then, I don't count that, because I'm performing.

And here's the downside: because I'm not a risk taker, I tend to stay in places longer than I should. I struggle to let things go. I often sit back and wonder, how different would my life look if I had been willing to take more risks?

So when I got let go from my job in September 2023, I couldn't say I was shocked. I was surprised by how and when it happened, but not that it happened at all. Truth is, God had already told me to leave a year earlier. And I didn't. I justified my disobedience by labeling it as responsibility. "I can't just leave without something else lined up, Lord. That's irresponsible. My bills are real, my obligations are real. I'm the executor of my own life." So I ignored His nudge.

Here's the tension I wrestled with: in church, we preach faith, but in the same breath we preach about having a Plan

"Okay God, I'll leave." On the other hand, I was secretly trying to store up enough money to float me until something else showed up. And every time I tried to save, something would happen that forced me to dip into the money. Then I tried to get another job—better pay, greater opportunities—but every door stayed shut.

Here's what I had to realize: backup plans don't belong in the same conversation as faith. There's wisdom in not leaving one thing until you have another when it's your decision. But when it's God's instruction? That's a different playing field. If He said leave, then there is no Plan B. There's only Plan Him.

Faith with a backup plan isn't faith at all. It's strategy. It's self-preservation. And it may work when man is in charge, but when God is in charge, His Word cannot fail. He's not a man that He should lie. If He said it, it has to come to pass. If He gave the command, then it has to work. Period. That's a nice shout in church, sure, but when you're actually living it out? It's terrifying. Because God doesn't ask you to do the logical, safe, or comfortable thing. He calls you into the radical, the outrageous, the thing that makes no earthly sense.

YOU WANT ME TO DO WHAT?

When I got to this section of Matthew 14, Peter stepping out of the boat, I can't help but see myself. Truth be told, I don't consider Peter or anyone else in that boat a risk taker. They weren't daredevils, adrenaline junkies, or "bet it all" type of guys. They were fishermen, and fishermen know water. They respect water. They know what can happen when you take it lightly. So, when Jesus came walking toward them and said, "It's me, don't be afraid," Peter asking, "Lord, if it's really you, tell me to come to you on the water,"—that's the moment I related to him. Because that's me. I always want confirmation. I'm always asking God for a sign.

But here's the kicker: we love asking God for a sign, and then when He gives us one, we act repulsed by it. "Lord, just show me it's You." And when He does, we start backpedaling. Jesus looked at Peter and essentially said, "Okay then. Here's your sign. Get out of the boat."

Now, let me just be real with you. That's where He would have lost me. Because what I know as fact is this: human beings sink in water. We don't walk on it. That's not even a debatable thing. That's science, gravity, physics—all the things that make sense in my analytical mind. So when Jesus says, "Walk on the water," I never would have got out of that boat. And that's what God does. He asks you to do something that sounds absolutely crazy. Something that doesn't line up with your education, your training, your logic, or your facts.

That wrestle—"Are you really asking me to do this?!"—is the same wrestle the widow woman faced in 2 Kings 4. This is what I call the Pourer's Plight. She had just a little bit of oil left, and God, through the prophet, told her to go borrow vessels from all her neighbors—not a few, but as many as she could get. Empty vessels at that! And then she was told to go inside, shut the door, and pour her little bit of oil into all those jars.

Do you see the ridiculousness of that command? What she was asked to do on top of what she was already dealing with seemed outrageous. It's the same frustration we feel when God asks us to move, obey, or give when we already feel depleted. She had to be sitting there like, "What?! How in the world am I supposed to pour into all of this when I barely have enough for myself?"

What God was really asking her to do was invest. To pour means to spend, to give out the whole of, to exhaust. And that's the plight of the pourer: obedience. Not pouring when you're full—that's easy. But pouring when you're empty. Worshiping when your heart is broken. Serving when your life is falling apart. Giving—not just money, but time, energy, love—when you're exhausted. That's the test.

And here's why faith is so hard: because faith is illogical. Faith doesn't make sense, but faith makes sense of it all. The moment God's command collides with human logic, you are thrust into the tension of faith. Hebrews 11:1 says it plainly: "Now faith is the substance of things hoped for, the evidence of things not seen." Faith literally sits in the middle of two present tenses and makes the sentence complete. Without faith, the thought falls apart.

But let me dismantle one of the biggest misconceptions about faith: faith does not rid you of reality. Faith doesn't pretend facts don't exist. Faith just offers you another reality to live by.

The reality of the world is governed by facts. The reality of the believer is governed by truth.

Facts are evidence. Facts are doctors' reports with X-rays and MRIs that show cancer. Facts are eviction notices giving you three days to come up with the full amount or get out. Facts are red numbers in your bank account. Facts are what you see.

But Jesus didn't call Himself "a fact." In John 14:6, He said, "I am the Way, the Truth, and the Life."

Facts can be checked, but Truth has to be encountered. Facts sit on paper, but Truth is a Person. And where we've been getting it wrong is that we've been treating facts like they are truth instead of taking the facts to the Truth.

We've been sitting around pity parties rehearsing facts, not realizing facts can't be trusted. Because facts change. The doctor can say cancer today and tomorrow the scan is clear. The bank can say overdraft today and tomorrow unexpected provision shows up. Facts shift. Truth doesn't. Truth is the same yesterday, today, and forevermore.

So the question becomes, whose report will you believe? Are you going to live by the facts or stand on the Truth?

Let me remind you: there was a day when facts and Truth had beef. The fact was Jesus died. That's what everybody saw. They nailed Him to a cross, pierced His side, and buried Him in a tomb. That's fact. Mary went to the tomb expecting fact to still be there. But when she arrived, she was met by the Truth, who asked her, "Why do you seek the living among the dead?"

The fact was He was crucified. The Truth was He got up.

And I've come to tell you: you may go searching for facts, but if you hang around long enough, you're going to run straight into the Truth.

That's why faith begins where your comfort zone ends. Faith begins where your facts stop making sense and the Truth steps in.

FIGHT THE HOOD FIGHT OF FAITH

So in order for us to fully embrace this idea that faith is about what Truth offers instead of what facts present, we have to pause and really define what faith actually is. We throw that word around in church so often that it starts to feel like spiritual slang. People treat faith like it's their own personal spiritual registry—like God is Amazon, and if you just have enough "faith points," He'll ship whatever you asked for straight to your doorstep. But faith is not your Make-a-Wish Foundation. Faith has zero to do with what you want, and everything to do with what He said.

That's the heart of it. I'm not healed because I want healing. I believe God to heal me because He said He would. And that's what makes Him faithful. Not that He bows to my preferences, but that He binds Himself to His promises.

My dad once told me something that stuck with me. He said, "A man is only as good as his word." And he drilled that into us sons—that if you say you're going to do something, you'd better do it, because trust lives or dies on whether or not you keep your word. That's how credibility is built. Now, if that's the logic of my natural father—an imperfect man—

then how much more do you think my Heavenly Father values His Word? He is incapable of lying. His reputation is on the line every time He speaks. And He will never let His Word fall flat.

That's why Romans 10:17 reminds us: "Faith comes by hearing, and hearing by the Word of God." Not by your Amazon wish list. Not by scrolling Instagram and coveting your neighbor's possessions. Not by daydreaming about what you think you deserve. Faith is only born out of hearing what God has said. That's the soil it grows in. And anything else—your desires, your ideas, your strategies—might produce ambition, but it won't produce faith.

This is the tension of faith, and especially of being in the middle. Faith in the middle is not some pretty, Instagrammable process. It's a fight. A fight to remember what He said when everything around you is screaming the opposite. A fight to believe in a Word when the facts don't line up. A fight to hold on to Truth when feelings are pulling you under.

I call it a hood fight. If you've ever seen a hood fight, you know it's not pretty. There are no rules, no referees, no weight classes. It's not elegant or strategic—it's by any means necessary. Hair pulling, shirt ripping, swinging wild, throwing whatever's in reach. Hood fights are about survival. And that's exactly what faith in the middle feels like sometimes. It's not polished, it's not clean, it's not even Instagram-worthy. It's scrappy. It's messy. It's waking up every morning saying, "I will not let go of what He said."

And here's the thing: faith in the middle is where you have to fight to preserve it. Faith in the middle doesn't just coast—you have to contend for it. Because you're pulled in two directions at once.

This is the fight:
What I see vs. What I know.
How it feels vs. What He said.

Faith is not pretending what I see isn't real. Faith is deciding what He said is more real.

Let me clarify it even further:

Faith is not a "make-a-wish foundation."

Faith is not about what I want, but about what God has spoken.

Faith is not bending His hand toward my will; prayer and supplication align my heart with His.

Faith is about anchoring myself in what He said, not in what I feel.

And let me encourage you with this picture: when the tide goes out, it doesn't mean the ocean has disappeared. Faith can feel that way sometimes—low, withdrawn, even empty—but the Source is still there. The ocean is still present, even if the waves have pulled back for a moment. And just like the tide always returns, the God who spoke will always bring His Word back to the surface.

That's why Jesus calling Peter out of the boat wasn't about proving Peter's bravery or stroking his ego. It was about testing whether he could believe what Jesus said over what he saw. Jesus said, "Come." That's it. And if the Son of God says "Come," then that one Word is enough to override every fact Peter knew about water, gravity, and drowning. But the wrestle is real—because faith demands that you trust the Word over your senses, the Truth over the facts.

And that, right there, is where I live most days. In the fight of faith.

ME... CAN YOU FOCUS ON ME...

By now, you already know I love good music. It's in my DNA. And if there's one thing about me, I'm going to find a soundtrack for my life moments. There's a song by H.E.R. that stops me in my tracks every time I hear it. It's called "Focus." In the song, she's crying out for full-fledged attention—"Can you focus on me?" And if there was ever a song that could score this scene with Peter walking on water, it would be that one.

When Peter finally steps out on the water, he's doing something nobody had ever done before. He is walking on the Word of Jesus. That one word—"Come"—had enough power in it to defy gravity, override logic, and carry him across a stormy sea. And for a few steps, Peter actually lives in that reality. He's walking, and as long as his eyes are on Jesus, he's standing in the impossible. But then it happens. The Bible says he saw the wind and became afraid.

Now here's the thing: the wind had been blowing the whole time. The storm didn't just appear the moment Peter stepped out of the boat. The waves didn't suddenly rise higher. The lightning didn't just start flashing. All of that was already there before he took his first step. The only thing that changed was his focus.

And when Peter's focus shifted, his faith faltered. Jesus caught him and asked a piercing question: "You of little faith, why did you doubt?" Notice Jesus didn't say, "You of no faith." Because Peter did have faith—it was faith that got him out of the boat in the first place. But Jesus called it little faith, not because of its size, but because of its distraction.

Doubt is really just distracted faith. It's faith that starts strong but then gets pulled in another direction. It's not that Peter didn't believe; it's that he stopped believing in the right thing. He shifted from trusting the Word he heard to being consumed by the sound of the wind.

And isn't that what we do? We start out convinced, walking on what God said. Then the distractions come. Bills pile up. The doctor's report comes back. People leave. Opportunities dry up. And before we know it, our focus has shifted from the Word that got us started to the noise that wants to take us under.

But here's the revelation: the same wind that didn't kill you before isn't going to kill you now. Think about it. That wind had been blowing against the boat all night, and the disciples were still alive. The waves had been crashing, and the boat hadn't sunk. The storm had been raging, but they were still standing. So why did Peter suddenly think the same storm that couldn't kill him then would be able to kill him now? That's what distraction does—it magnifies what's happening around you and minimizes what's already been proven to sustain you.

And Jesus' question—"Why did you doubt?"—is really another way of asking, "Why did you let distraction rob you of your focus? Why did you shift your weight from My Word back onto your fears? Why did you trust the storm more than you trusted Me?"

That's the sting of doubt. It convinces us that what's happening around us is more important than what He already said to us. But the storm has no authority to cancel His Word. The wind has no power to overturn His promise. The waves may roar, but His "Come" still holds.

That's why faith has to be fiercely guarded from distraction. Faith isn't just believing once and then coasting. Faith is maintaining focus in the middle of noise. Faith is refusing to let what you see drown out what He said. Faith is stubbornly saying, "I know what the facts are, but I choose to trust the Truth."

When Peter cried out, "Lord, save me!" Jesus immediately reached out His hand and caught him. And this is what I love about Jesus: even when our faith is distracted, He doesn't let us drown. Even when we lose focus, He's still faithful. Even when we let doubt creep in, He still shows up as Rescuer.

So the question becomes less about whether the storm will take you under and more about whether you'll stay focused long enough to keep walking through it. Because the storm was never the issue. The issue was always focus.

IMMEDIATELY JESUS REACHED OUT HIS HAND AND CAUGHT HIM....

MATTHEW 14:31 (NIV)

That one sentence in Matthew has carried me for years. Because Jesus didn't let Peter sink. He didn't stand back and watch to see how far Peter would go down. He didn't shake His head and say, "Well, I told you to keep your eyes on Me." No, the moment Peter began to sink, Jesus reached out His hand. That's what a Father does. That's what love does. He saves you before you drown. And when I think about that moment, it always reminds me of a run-in I had with my dad not too long ago.

To give weight to that parallel, you have to understand my backstory. I didn't grow up with my biological father. In fact, I didn't grow up with any man consistently serving in the role of "father" in my life. I didn't even meet my real dad until I was twenty-five years old. Up until then, I thought another man was my father—because that's what my mom told me. Then in 2017, the truth came out. The man I had been calling "Dad" all my life wasn't my biological father. I found out the name of the man who was, and like any millennial would, I took to Google. Within minutes, I had found him. He lived in the same city as me all along. I had brothers. I had sisters. A whole family I never knew existed.

I sat down and wrote him a message. I didn't want to overwhelm him or demand anything from him. So I typed, "Hey, I know you don't know me, and I'm scared to even send this message. But I was told that you are my biological father. I'm twenty-five years old. I'm in a stable place in my life. I'm not asking for anything from you except a meeting to discuss this and to seek out the truth." He was hesitant at first—and I can't even fault him. Our lives had already been moving in different directions, and he didn't want to disrupt what had already been established. But then he met me, and immediately he saw—well, he saw himself. I was his twin. The resemblance was undeniable. We followed through and got bloodwork, and the results confirmed what we both already knew in our hearts: he was my father.

From that day forward, he accepted me into the fold. I went from being Josh to being son. That moment changed everything—but let me be clear, it wasn't without its challenges. We didn't know each other. We didn't have shared history. We came from different contexts, different backgrounds. He didn't understand me, and I was struggling to learn him. We went through a season of trying to make up for lost time, but eventually we realized we couldn't rewrite the past. What we could do was build from where we were. And that's what we did. That's my dad, and I love him real bad.

Recently, my siblings and I were over at his house having a great time. As the evening wound down and it was time to leave, he walked us all out to our cars like he always does. For some reason, I'm usually the last one to leave. Maybe it's because I'm the oldest boy, or maybe it's just our rhythm, but that's our time to have father-son conversation. Normally, those moments are light—we recap the night, laugh about the gathering, and share a good word before parting ways. But this time was different.

This time, he stopped me. He looked me directly in the eyes and said something I will never forget. He said, "Out of all my kids, you're the most independent. I don't hear from you when you're going through. And I get it—you like to figure things out. But hear me: no child of mine has to go without. You have a father who will help you. I'm here to help you. I don't want you to think that because you're the newest one here, you don't get the same privileges. You are my son too."

I was flabbergasted. I had no words. Because I didn't know I could do that. I didn't know I could lean on a father.

My response to him was simple: "I figure things out on my own because I don't know how to have a father."

And that moment hit me like a revelation. That's the struggle so many of us carry in faith—we don't know how to receive Fatherhood. We know how to be independent. We know how to figure things out. We know how to grind, push, endure, and survive. But we don't always know how to rest in the care of a Father. We don't always know how to call for help and believe He will answer.

Here's the truth: faith flourishes when you know you have a Father who cares for you. When you know you don't have to figure it all out alone. When you know you don't have to sink, because even if you do, His hand is already reaching for you. That's why Jesus didn't let Peter drown. He saved him—not just for Peter's sake, but for His name's sake. Because that's what a good Father does.

That moment with my dad made me realize something even deeper about the nature of fatherhood. Fathers don't just care about the needs of their children—they care about the legacy of their name. My dad wasn't just saying, "I'll help you because you're struggling." He was saying, "I'll help you because you bear my name now. You're mine. And no child of mine is going to be left without." It wasn't just about provision; it was about identity. His reputation as a father was tied to how well he covered his son.

And if that's true for my earthly father, a man with flaws and failures just like anyone else, how much more is it true for our Heavenly Father? God's name is on us. Scripture tells us that *He leads us in paths of righteousness for His name's sake* (Psalm 23:3). That means His faithfulness to us is not only about our survival—it's about His glory. When He saves, when He provides, when He rescues, He's showing the world that His Word cannot fail and that His name cannot be tarnished.

That's why Jesus didn't let Peter drown. If Peter went under, it would have looked like Jesus' Word—"Come"—

wasn't enough to hold him. And God's Word cannot return void. He had to save Peter, not just for Peter's life, but for the integrity of His name. And that's what you need to know about your faith walk: when you belong to Him, He doesn't just move for you—He moves for His reputation. He moves so that the world will see He is exactly who He says He is.

That's blessed reassurance. That's what steadies me in my storms. Because sometimes I don't have enough faith to stand on my own. Sometimes my focus drifts. Sometimes I get distracted by the wind and the waves. But He still reaches down. Not because I've always gotten it right, not because my faith has been flawless, but because His name is on me.

And that's the tension of being a child of God: you're not just carrying your own story, you're carrying His. He saves you for His name's sake. He delivers you so the world will see that He is Deliverer. He heals you so people will know He is Healer. He provides for you so the nations will testify that He is Jehovah Jireh. His reputation is wrapped up in your redemption.

And that truth changes everything about how I see faith. Faith is not about begging God to move; faith is about standing on the certainty that He will, because He can't afford not to. His Word is on the line. His glory is on the line. His name is on the line.

So when Jesus reached for Peter, it wasn't just compassion—it was covenant. It was a Father saying, "I've got you, because you belong to Me. My hand is always stronger than your sinking." That's why I can rest in faith even when I don't have it all figured out. Because at the end of the day, my faith doesn't save me. My Father does.

And this is where the chapter comes full circle. Peter's story wasn't about him being fearless, flawless, or even consistent. Peter's story was about Jesus. Because the headline isn't that Peter sank—it's that Jesus didn't let him drown. The lesson wasn't that Peter walked perfectly; the lesson was that when Peter fell, Jesus reached out His hand and saved him. That's blessed reassurance.

Faith, at its core, isn't about never wavering. It's not about living so steady that you never flinch at the storm. Faith isn't flawless. Faith is focused. Faith is the decision to keep your eyes on Jesus even when everything else is demanding your attention. And when your focus drifts, faith is crying out, *"Lord, save me!"* and knowing He will.

That's the comfort we carry in the middle: no word from God fails. If He said it, it has to happen. If He promised it, it has to come to pass. His Word is the most reliable force in the universe. Wind may shift, waves may crash, storms may roar—but His Word remains.

And more than that, He rescues you for His Name's sake. You are not just living for yourself—you are living under His banner. His reputation is tied to your redemption. He delivers you not only because you need saving, but because His glory is revealed when He saves. Every time He pulls you up, He proves again that His hand is stronger than your storm.

So what does that mean for you, right here, right now? It means you don't need a Plan B when your Father is Plan A. It means you can stop trying to engineer backup strategies in case God fails you—because He won't. It means you can silence the voices of fear, anxiety, and doubt that tell you the storm is bigger than your Savior. It means you can live in blessed reassurance: that no matter how fierce the wind, no matter how loud the waves, no matter how weak your faith feels in the moment, the hand of Jesus is never too far away.

Peter walked on water, but more importantly, he walked with the Word. And when he sank, the Word saved him. That's the essence of faith. Not perfection. Not control. Not having every answer mapped out. Just trust in the One who always shows up, always holds you, and always pulls you through.

So step out. Trust Him. Keep your eyes locked in. And when your focus slips, when your faith falters, when you feel yourself sinking, remember the blessed reassurance: His hand will always reach you before the water does.

Faith isn't flawless — it's focused. Focused on the hand that refuses to let you go. Even when you slip, His grip is stronger.

"I'M GLAD TO STILL BE HERE... BUT NOBODY KNOWS HOW HARD IT'S BEEN TO STILL BE HERE."

HEY GOD,

AM I WASTING MY TIME?

God, I have questions.
All of them, actually.
I know we're taught not to question You—but I've never really played by the rules.
And my questions aren't to challenge You... I'm just desperate for answers.
Because I'm trying.
I'm making efforts.
But I feel disappointed.
I feel like I missed it. I feel like I don't have what it takes.
I feel all of that today.
Sometimes I feel like Twinkie Clark when she wrote "Is my living in vain? Am I wasting my time?"
Those are real feelings. Real emotions.
Just because I'm saved, just because I believe and love You, doesn't mean I don't feel that.
But Twinkie didn't stop there—she kept singing: "No, of course not. It's not all in vain."
And maybe I should believe that too...
But right now, I'm not sure if I do.

So here are my questions.
When does all of this get better? Does it ever turn around for me? When does my door open? When does joy show up for real? Does my life really matter—or am I just a pawn? Did I miss it? Did I make up what I thought I heard and saw?

What does any of this even mean? The trauma, the disappointment, the heartbreak, the ache— what's the point?

Why does it feel like You snatched my support system away? And how am I supposed to trust anyone new, when I don't know how long they'll stay? Am I even in the right place? What am I supposed to be doing? Was what You showed me real? If it wasn't... please don't let me waste my time. Do I ever win? Do I ever get chosen? Do I ever become a father? Are You pleased with me?

It's been hard for a long time.
How much longer will it be like this?
Is my faith even good enough?
Why was this my path?
Wasn't there another way?
How does all of this pan out?
Is there anything left here for me?
Or am I only staying because it's all I know?
And one last thing...
Do I get to quit—peacefully—if it just gets to be too much?

8.
WHEN

When I was a kid, my granny ran what we called a candy house. If you grew up in the hood, you already know what that is. For us, it wasn't a corner store, but it might as well have been. Granny kept everything in there—chips, sodas, cookies, pickles, frozen cups, and of course, candy. And one of my favorites was Now & Laters. That little square of chewy fruit goodness was more than just a snack; it was an experience. We'd stuff our pockets with them, especially on the days when the adults forced us outside. You could count on a Now & Later to last you through the curb-ball games, the arguments over whose turn it was at riding the bike, or even just sitting in the tree talking about nothing. The thing about Now & Laters was they had a progression: you popped one in, and at first, it was hard—almost like a little brick. But if you were patient, it softened, the flavor came rushing out, and you could chew on it for a good while.

And when I think about those Now & Laters, I think about relationships—how sometimes we want everything to be soft and sweet right away, but real connection takes time. Someone once asked me what I thought was the downfall of relationships. Most people will quickly answer, "communication." And while I won't deny communication is important, I'd argue the deeper issue is comprehension. Communication is just words, but comprehension is understanding. It's possible for someone to talk all day and the other person not get it. But when comprehension shows up, meaning is exchanged, and connection takes root. Comprehension—the ability to understand the meaning of what is being read or heard—isn't just important for academics or careers. It's vital for relationships. It allows you to grasp what's being said, make connections, and think critically about what's in front of you. Without comprehension, you may hear the sound, but you'll miss the song.

And it's the same with God. Trusting God in seasons of uncertainty can only be done when you have the proper understanding. If all you have is communication—His Word—you might hear it but not comprehend it. You might repeat it but not receive it. Understanding shifts things. Understanding anchors you when everything around you is moving.

Because here's the truth you may not want to hear: you're going to always be in transition. Literally, your whole life will be defined by transition. Places change, spaces shift, people come and go, jobs open and close, desires rise and fall. Transition is not an interruption to your story; it is the story. It is literally built into creation. When God separated light from darkness and established day and night, He also created transition—and then He called it good. The sunrise and the sunset are transitions. The tide going out and coming back in is transition. The child learning to walk is transition. It's all part of the rhythm of life God set in motion. So why do we treat transition like it's punishment when God says it's part of His plan?

We've got to change how we view transition. God will throw your life into things without your permission—not because He's careless, but because He's committed to belief and glory. Think about when Jesus healed the blind man and people asked, "Who sinned, this man or his parents?" Jesus answered, "Neither. This happened so that the works of God might be displayed in him." In other words, "This wasn't about cause; it was about glory." Some of the transitions you've hated weren't about you at all. They were about showing others the God you trust. Your discomfort became their testimony. God gets the glory.

But here's the tension: we want understanding to be a "Now" thing, when most times it's a "Later" thing. We want clarity up front, answers on the first day, and explanations before we say yes. But that's not how God works. With Him, it's often Now & Later. You may not understand it now, but later it'll make sense. You may not see the fruit now, but later it'll show. Understanding is often delayed gratification.

And here's where the candy ties back in. Now & Laters are hard at first. They'll even hurt your teeth if you try to rush it. But give it time, and it softens. Then comes the burst of intense fruit flavor. Then comes the long-lasting chew. Then you realize that the hard beginning was part of what made it last longer than other candy. Isn't that just like God? The "hard now" is what sets you up for the "soft later." The beginning feels tough, but the resolve it produces makes the fruit of it last.

So the next time you're in transition and you don't understand, remember—your life is more like a Now & Later than a lollipop. Now it may be hard, but later it will get soft and easy. Now it may feel flavorless, but later the richness will come rushing out. Now it may feel like you don't get it, but later you'll see how every piece fit together. God's goal is not to make you comfortable; it's to make you convinced. Not to give you quick candy, but to grow you into someone who can endure.

When it comes to how we process life, human logic almost always defaults to "if." If this happens, then maybe I'll do that. If I get the job, I'll feel stable. If they stay with me, I'll finally feel secure. If the doctor's report changes, then I'll really believe God is good. If is the language of contingency, chance, and doubt. It leaves us suspended between possibility and fear, never quite anchored, because it is built on conditions we cannot control. "If" is fragile. "If" is shaky ground. It gives voice to uncertainty, to the fear that maybe things won't work out, maybe God won't come through, maybe life won't bend in our favor.

But the Kingdom of God does not operate in the currency of if. Heaven speaks a different language—the language of "when." "When" is rooted in certainty, timing, and sovereignty. "When" doesn't question God's ability; it simply waits on God's appointment. "When" is the assurance that the outcome has already been secured, even if the manifestation is still on its way. With God, there is no if I can but always when I will. Jesus never looked at a blind man and said, "If I can heal you." He said, "Receive your sight." He never told His disciples, "If I rise again." He said, "When I rise again." The difference is everything. If is built on human fragility, but when is built on divine finality.

Proverbs 13:12 frames this tension so beautifully: "Hope deferred makes the heart sick, but a longing fulfilled is a tree of life." We know what it feels like when hope gets delayed—it weighs on the heart, makes the spirit heavy, and wears down our endurance. Deferred hope is discouraging. But when the "when" of God finally collides with the longing of our soul, it becomes a tree of life—fruitful, grounding, nourishing, alive. Notice that it doesn't say a longing fulfilled is a quick snack or a fleeting relief; it says it's a tree, something rooted, established, and life-giving.

That's what your "when" moment is. It is the collision point between God's sovereignty and your expectation. It's when the waiting, the confusion, the transition, and even the disappointment suddenly make sense because they were all carrying you toward fulfillment. Your "when" is not just an answered prayer; it's the moment new life begins to branch out in you. And once you've lived through the "if" seasons and seen God bring you into your "when," you carry an unshakable resolve. Because after you've tasted the fruit of a fulfilled promise, it becomes impossible to go back to doubting if God can.

WHEN JESUS ANSWERED, "YOU DO NOT KNOW NOW WHAT I AM DOING, BUT LATER YOU WILL UNDERSTAND."

JOHN 13:7 (NRSV)

I was sitting one day just chillin, having a conversation with God, when He did what He always does—pulled out the mirror. You ever sit down with Him expecting comfort, and He slides conviction across the table instead? That's what happened. He looked at me and said, "Take a deep breath, because what I'm about to tell you is going to sting: you're breaking your own heart and inflicting your own pain."

Of course, I pushed back. "Absolutely not, Lord. I don't even have the power to do that to myself. How am I doing that?" And His response hit me like a ton of bricks: "Your need for carnal understanding is ruining your life. You're trying so hard to understand it that you're destroying yourself."

John 13:7 leapt off the page at me in that moment. "Jesus answered, 'You do not know now what I am doing, but later you will understand.'" And that one verse became a lifeline, because in it Jesus reveals the truth about how He operates. He divides life into two categories: now and later. There are things you will never grasp in the now, because the now is too small for the weight of the revelation. There are things you will only grasp later, when the Spirit has expanded your capacity to understand.

Let me bring some context to that verse. At this point in the Gospel of John, Jesus is washing the feet of His disciples. The text tells us, "Jesus knew His hour had come." In other words, He was fully aware of the bigger picture, even when they were not. He bends down with a towel and begins to wash their feet, and immediately the disciples push back: "Whoa, whoa, my guy... this isn't how it goes around here.

What are you doing?" They couldn't wrap their minds around it, because it didn't fit the framework of what they understood a rabbi, a teacher, or a king to do.

Catch this: Jesus was doing a good thing, but it was a new thing. And because it was new, it felt foreign. And because it felt foreign, it felt wrong. But the truth was, nothing was wrong—it was just unfamiliar. Isn't that how we live sometimes? God begins to do something in our lives that we've never experienced before, and we confuse our discomfort with danger. The brain is wired for survival, so when it doesn't have a reference point, it assumes a threat.

Now, let's walk through three things tucked inside this one verse in John 13:7—three things Jesus reveals about the tension between now and later. There's a problem, clarity, and a promise.

THE PROBLEM – "YOU DO NOT KNOW"

The first thing Jesus does is confront perception. He doesn't sugarcoat it; He comes out swinging: "You do not know." That word "know" in this text translates to "perception." Jesus was basically saying, "What you think you know, you don't. The way you're reading this moment is completely off."

And isn't that the problem? Our perception may feel valid, but that doesn't make it true. You can have a perspective that feels justified by your pain, your logic, or your history, but still be reading it wrong. And when your perception is off, your behavior follows. You pull back. You stop showing up. You lose consistency—not because God changed, but because your perspective did.

Look at Lazarus. When Jesus finally showed up after Lazarus had died, Martha ran to Him with her perception. "Lord, had you been here, my brother would not have died." Translation: From where I stand, this is Your fault. And can we be real? Some of us are standing in the way of our worship because we've been silently disappointed with God. You prayed. You fasted. You sent word. And He didn't show up the way you thought He would. And now, like Martha, you're reading this all wrong.

But here's the mercy of Jesus—He doesn't leave us with just the problem. He responds with clarity.

THE CLARITY – "IT'S ME"

Jesus looks at Martha and basically says, "You're talking about resurrection like it's a date on your calendar. Nah fam, I am the resurrection. You don't need to wait for a day; you need to look at Me. It's not an event; it's a person."

This is where clarity enters: You don't need to understand it, you need to understand Him. Understanding Him changes everything. When you understand Him, you realize He has no ill intent toward you. His plans are not to harm you but to prosper you. When you understand Him, you stop mislabeling His presence as absence, His process as punishment, His method as malice.

But notice something—Mary wasn't even in the room yet. The one who used to sit at His feet was now distant. And doesn't that happen to us? When we get disappointed, when things don't go the way we expected, suddenly worship is hard. The hands that used to lift freely get heavy. The mouth that used to sing without prompting grows silent. Why? Because we're so focused on the what that we've lost sight of the Who.

Mary comes in later and says the same thing as Martha: "Lord, had you been here..." And Jesus hears the pain but pushes past it: "Didn't I tell you that if you believed, you would see the glory of God?" Translation: Your perception has agreement, but agreement doesn't make it truth. Just because multiple people see it the same way doesn't mean it's right.

And that's the clarity some of us need right now. The pain is real. The confusion is real. But the truth is higher than your perception: this is His doing. And if it's His doing, then you can trust His intent. He's not trying to kill you—He's curating your belief.

THE PROMISE – "LATER YOU WILL UNDERSTAND"

And here's where it lands: Jesus doesn't just confront the problem or offer clarity; He gives a promise. "Later you will understand." Not now. Later. Which means this moment is not the end. Which means you've got to keep contending. Which means there's a revelation on the other side of what you're going through.

In a little while, God is going to give you an "Ahhhh, I got it now" moment. That's the promise. That's the tree of life Proverbs 13 talks about—the longing fulfilled that makes all the waiting worth it.

But hear me: if you keep forcing your limited brain to comprehend the limitless God, you'll keep wounding yourself. In order to serve Him, you can't serve your own understanding. Your understanding has to be made holy. Your peace is on the other side of surrendering your need to understand.

The goal of this season is not to kill you; it's to get you to surrender. And I don't just mean surrender the stuff people can see—the habits, the public struggles, the big obvious sins. I mean surrender the small foxes too. Surrender the need to understand it. Because if you buck against what He's doing simply because you don't understand, what you're really saying is, "You're not Lord over me."

Jesus washing the disciples' feet was new and uncomfortable. Martha and Mary losing Lazarus felt cruel and unfair. But in both situations, the truth remained: He knew something they did not know. He was orchestrating something their perception couldn't perceive.

And here's the truth about understanding: you don't need to understand it. Please don't lose your understanding of Him.

Job has always fascinated me, because his story is the textbook case of what it means to live through something you do not understand. If anybody had a reason to be angry, confused, or disappointed with God, it was Job. In one sweep of tragedy, he lost his wealth, his health, and his children. And if that wasn't enough, he had a wife telling him to "curse God and die," and friends who were supposed to comfort him but instead spent chapter after chapter giving him bad theology. Job is sitting in ashes, scraping his sores, asking the same question we all ask in the middle of storms: What is going on?

But here's where Job teaches us something profound. For most of the book, he goes back and forth with God. He vents, he argues, he tries to make sense of it. His perception tells him, "This is unfair. This is wrong. This is punishment." And if you read him carefully, you can feel how his perception shapes his behavior—he gets defensive, he tries to justify himself, he even starts talking in circles because he wants to understand it.

And then God speaks. Not with answers. Not with a map. Not even with comfort in the way we think of comfort. God speaks out of the whirlwind, essentially saying, "Were you there when I laid the foundations of the earth? Do you give the horse its strength? Do you send lightning bolts on their way? Job, you're demanding answers, but you don't know enough to demand them. You want to understand it, but you don't understand Me."

And something shifts in Job right there. He stops arguing. He stops demanding. He stops scraping for comprehension. He says in Job 42:2–5, "I know that You can do all things; no purpose of Yours can be thwarted... My ears had heard of You, but now my eyes have seen You."

That right there is resolve. It's the moment he moves from perception to revelation. He doesn't get an explanation, but he gets an encounter. And the encounter convinces him. He essentially says, "I am convinced. I don't understand it, but I understand You. And that's enough."

And notice what happens after Job resolves who God is: the text says God restored him, gave him double for his trouble. But here's what we miss sometimes—the double wasn't the prize. The double was the fruit. The real prize was the revelation. The real breakthrough was Job saying, "I am convinced." Because when you're convinced about Him, you don't need every "it" to line up. You stop needing God to perform on your terms, because you've become anchored in His character.

I think that's where most of us miss it. We keep thinking the destination is the blessing, the breakthrough, the answered prayer, the dry land. But Job proves the destination is actually resolve. The destination is when you can stand in the middle of unanswered questions, in the middle of pain you don't have a category for, and say, "Yet I trust Him. Yet I know Him. Yet I am convinced."

See, it's not about getting to the place that flows with milk and honey. It's about knowing the God of the milk and honey. It's not about reaching Gennesaret and calling it a garden of riches. It's about realizing that gardens don't grow overnight, and true riches aren't money—they're rootedness, conviction, endurance, and peace. And all of that only sprouts after you come through a season of not understanding it but holding on to Him.

That's why I love Paul in Romans 8. He echoes Job's resolve when he says, "We know that in all things God works for the good of those who love Him, who have been called according to His purpose." And if you keep reading, Paul defines what that good really is—it's not comfort, it's conformity. It's not ease, it's image. The good is that we would be conformed to the likeness of His Son. Which means even suffering, even confusion, even silence has an assignment.

And this is the part that wrecks me: Job's double portion didn't erase the grief of his losses. It didn't magically undo the pain of burying his children. Pain was part of his story. But revelation reframed it. Resolve redeemed it. Because once he was convinced of who God is, even his suffering became seed. And when seed dies, it produces more.

So maybe your life right now feels like Job's ashes. Maybe you've been scraping at your pain, trying to make sense of it, trying to figure out what you did wrong. Maybe people around you have been quick to diagnose your suffering and slow to simply sit with you in it. And maybe, just maybe, God isn't going to give you an explanation. Maybe He's going to give you Himself. And maybe that will be enough to get you to say what Job said: "I am convinced."

Because when you realize Who is with you, that's when you've arrived at the place called Beautiful. The destination isn't a location. The destination is conviction. The sign of arrival isn't dry land under your feet. It's dry land in you. It's when the waves don't move you anymore. It's when the storm no longer defines you. It's when you can look at unanswered prayers, unfulfilled dreams, and unexpected pain and still say, "But I trust Him."

And that's when you'll discover the real miracle—that broken pieces still float. That even if the boat doesn't make it, you will. That the goal was never to give you certainty, but to anchor you in surrender. And when you surrender, you'll realize that even when you don't understand it, you'll always understand Him.

THEN THOSE WHO WERE IN THE BOAT WORSHIPED HIM, SAYING, "TRULY YOU ARE THE SON OF GOD."

MATTHEW 14:33 (NIV)

When the storm finally calmed in Matthew 14, the disciples weren't left clapping for the waves or applauding the wind for dying down. Their attention wasn't on the boat, or even on the fact that they had survived. What captured them was the man standing in the middle of it all. Scripture says they bowed down and confessed, "Truly You are the Son of God."

That moment matters because it shifts the spotlight. The revelation was never about understanding the storm—it was about understanding the One who commands it. Up until then, they had seen Jesus heal bodies, multiply bread, and even silence a storm with His words, but there was still something they didn't quite grasp. It wasn't until this moment, when He pulled Peter up from sinking and stepped back into the boat, that their perception changed. They finally saw Him not just as a teacher, not just as a miracle worker, but as the Son of God.

And that's the whole point of storms. Not that you would come out with a weather report of what happened, but that you would come out with a revelation of who He is. The goal isn't that you'd become an expert in reading the wind, but that you'd know the voice that calms it. Because storms will always be part of life. Some come quick and pass fast, others rage longer than you think you can handle. But if all you learn from a storm is how bad it was, you've missed it. The real lesson is seeing who was with you in it.

The disciples didn't walk away saying, "That was the worst storm we've ever been through." They walked away saying, "We've just discovered who He truly is." That's the kind of revelation storms are designed to give you—not an understanding of it but an understanding of Him.

One of the most freeing shifts you can ever make in the middle of life's storms is this: stop calling it struggling, and start calling it what it really is—being between miracles. Think about it. You've already witnessed God do something before, and if you're still breathing, it means He's not done yet. That space you're in, the tension, the waiting, the confusion—it's not wasted space. It's between space. It's not the end of the story; it's the middle where the miracle you saw last and the miracle you're becoming next overlap.

That changes everything. Because "struggling" makes it sound like I'm losing. "Struggling" makes it sound like I don't have enough faith, like I'm drowning under the weight of everything. But when I reframe it and say, "I'm not struggling; I'm just in between miracles," I start to see this moment differently. This is not punishment, it's preparation. This is not God ignoring me, it's God shaping me.

And that's really what the storm was about for Peter and the disciples. The test was never about breaking them down—it was about reshaping their minds concerning Him. Jesus didn't pull Peter out of the water to humiliate him; He pulled him up so that Peter could see Him differently. The waves weren't meant to drown them; they were meant to deliver a revelation. And when that revelation hit—when the disciples could say, "Truly, You are the Son of God"—that was the pass mark of the test.

That's what storms are: open-book tests designed not to measure your strength but to deepen your revelation. You don't pass because you came out dry. You don't pass because the boat held together. You pass when your understanding of who He is becomes stronger than your memory of how bad it felt. You pass when you can stand in the middle of transition and declare, "He's still Lord. He's still with me. He's still God."

So maybe you're in that in-between space right now. You've seen Him work before, but you're not yet standing in the next miracle. Don't mislabel it as struggle. Call it what it is: the sacred space between miracles. Because that's the place where your perception shifts, where your faith matures, and where your revelation of Him becomes the miracle you carry forward.

MORE THAN A DESTINATION...

When the boat finally touched down after the storm, Matthew says they landed at Gennesaret. Now, if you skip past that too quickly, you'll miss something rich. The name Gennesaret literally means "Garden of Riches." That's not just a throwaway detail—it's a revelation. Because gardens don't spring up overnight. Gardens require time. Gardens require cultivation. Gardens require pruning, planting, waiting, watering, and a whole lot of patience.

So when Scripture says they landed at Gennesaret, it's not just telling us a geographical location—it's giving us a picture of what this journey was always meant to produce. Notice, it doesn't say "Bouquet of Riches" or "Plant of Riches." It says Garden. And a garden is layered. A garden grows in stages. A garden is something that keeps producing long after the seed has been planted.

That tells me that the destination God is trying to get you to is not a moment, not a single answered prayer, not a one-time blessing. It's a garden. It's something lasting, sustaining, and expansive. See, some of us want God to give us bouquets—quick fixes, pretty arrangements we can hold up for a picture. But bouquets fade. Gardens feed generations. Gardens outlive storms. Gardens turn seasons into cycles of life.

And let's also be clear: when the text says "Garden of Riches," it is not talking about money. Riches in the Kingdom don't look like dollar signs. Riches are revelation.

Riches are peace that doesn't crack under pressure. Riches are conviction that can't be shaken. Riches are faith that remains when logic runs out. That's why Paul could say, "Oh, the depth of the riches of the wisdom and knowledge of God!" (Romans 11:33). True riches are found in what you know of Him.

Think about it—what good is a million dollars if you lose your mind in the storm? What good is a promotion if you still can't sleep at night? What good is recognition if you don't know who you are? The storm wasn't designed to get them to a place of more money or more status. It was designed to cultivate in them a garden of riches that no thief could steal, no storm could wash away, and no enemy could uproot.

That's the beauty of Gennesaret. It reminds us that God doesn't deal in microwaves; He deals in gardens. He doesn't rush harvests; He works through process. And when you land in the place He's bringing you to, it won't just be something for you to enjoy in the moment—it'll be something you can cultivate, nurture, and watch multiply.

So here's the challenge for us: stop despising the slowness of your process. Stop treating the middle like it's wasted space. Gardens take time, but they're worth it. What God is building in you is not a quick arrangement; it's a garden. He's not handing you something to show off for a season— He's rooting something in you that will outlast the storm you just came through.

That's why the landing place matters. Because when you step onto the soil of Gennesaret, you realize the real miracle wasn't just making it through the storm. The real miracle was what the storm planted in you. And once it takes root, it becomes a garden you can draw from for the rest of your life.

When I think about what it really means to "arrive," I'm reminded of Acts 3. Peter and John are on their way to the temple to pray, and at the gate sits a man who had been lame since birth. Every day, his friends carried him to that same spot, and every day he begged for coins. For him, survival meant asking for small help to get through another 24 hours. His whole expectation of life had been reduced to loose change. And the irony of it all? He was stationed at the gate called Beautiful.

Think about that. A man who had never walked a day in his life sat at the threshold of beauty but couldn't enter into it. He was close to it but never in it. That's what disappointment and delay will do to you—it'll have you living on the edge of beautiful, but never experiencing it for yourself. And when Peter and John approached, the man looked at them expecting the usual—coins, something temporary, something small enough to keep him alive but not big enough to change his life.

But God always exceeds expectation. Peter looks at him and says, "Silver and gold I do not have, but what I do have I give you. In the name of Jesus Christ of Nazareth, walk." In that moment, the lame man's entire world shifted. He didn't get coins—he got strength. He didn't just get survival—he got restoration. And for the first time, he entered into the very place he had only ever sat outside of. The gate wasn't just a landmark anymore—it became a doorway into a new way of living.

That's the power of revelation: when you realize Who is with you, that's when you arrive at the place called Beautiful. The man thought his miracle was money, but God gave him Himself. And that's what arriving really is—it's not about geography, status, or finally getting your "big break." It's about understanding who Jesus is in the middle of your life. Because once you know Who is with you, you can finally walk into places you've been sitting outside of for years.

Which brings me to this: what's the true sign of arrival? Too often, we think it's about what's under our feet—dry land, stability, a place where nothing shifts anymore. But the older I get, the more I realize it's not about dry land beneath you; it's about dry land within you. It's not about external stability; it's about internal resolve.

Because let's be honest: the storms don't stop. Life doesn't suddenly smooth out into perfect weather. The wind still blows, the waves still rise, people still leave, jobs still change, and seasons still shift. If you keep waiting on life to stop storming before you declare you've arrived, you'll be waiting forever. Arrival is not a matter of circumstance—it's a matter of the soul. It's when you can stand in the middle of chaos and still be steady on the inside.

Resolve is greater than location. Inner stillness is greater than outer circumstances. That's why Paul could write in Romans 8:28–29, "And we know that in all things God works for the good of those who love Him, who have been called according to His purpose. For those God foreknew He also predestined to be conformed to the image of His Son." Most of us stop at verse 28 and shout over "all things working together for my good." But Paul doesn't stop there. He clarifies what the real good is in verse 29—not just things working out in your favor, but you being conformed into the image of Christ.

That changes everything. Because if the goal is image, then even the storms serve a purpose. Even the waiting works. Even the pain produces something. The good isn't about comfort; it's about conformity. The good isn't about landing in a place; it's about becoming someone.

So the real sign you've made it is not the storm stopping. It's you stopping—your panic, your striving, your desperate need to control. The real sign is peace on the inside, even when there's none on the outside. It's dry land within you. That's when you know you've arrived. Not because the boat held together. Not because the wind finally died down. But because you've discovered a stillness inside yourself that matches the stillness of the God who walks on waves.

THE BOAT MAY NOT MAKE IT WITH YOU

Here's the thing I need you to see: sometimes the boat doesn't make it. That little vessel you thought was holding your life together—your plans, your strategies, your safety nets, your routines—it might not survive the storm. The disciples didn't always make it to shore with the boat intact, and neither will you. And that's okay. Because the miracle was never in the boat. The miracle was in you.

Paul paints this picture so clearly in Acts 27. A violent storm batters the ship carrying him to Rome, and the sailors panic. They throw cargo overboard. They try to lighten the load. They do everything human logic says to do. But Paul stands up and delivers a word that should echo in your heart: "The ship will be destroyed, but not one of you will lose your life." In the end, the vessel didn't make it, but the people did. Some swam to shore. Others clung to broken planks and fragments of the ship. But here's the line that shouts across generations: broken pieces still float.

That's the hope of the gospel right there. Even if what was carrying you doesn't make it, you will. Even if your plans fall apart, you will. Even if your expectations crumble into fragments, you will. Because Jesus didn't come to save the boat; He came to save you. He didn't promise the structure would survive—He promised you would arrive.

So let me free you: stop obsessing over keeping the boat together. Stop trying to duct-tape what God already said would break. Stop grieving the loss of things you were never meant to carry to shore. Boats are temporary. Your destiny is eternal. God isn't preserving your plans—He's preserving your purpose.

And that's why the middle matters. The middle is not wasted. The storm is not pointless. The test is not cruel. Every gust of wind, every crashing wave, every sleepless night, every unanswered question—it's all been pushing you toward revelation. Revelation of Him. Revelation that stabilizes you when everything else is unstable. Revelation that matures your faith from "if" to "when," from perception to truth, from panic to peace.

This is the resolve of the middle: "Even if the boat doesn't make it, I will. Even if it's broken pieces, I will float. Even if I don't understand it, I still understand Him. Even if everything around me is shaking, there is dry land inside of me." That's what it means to pass the test. Not that you come out with everything you started with, but that you come out with a greater revelation of the One who was with you all along.

So as you close this book, let me speak this into your spirit: Your middle is not your end. You're not stuck; you're stationed. You're not drowning; you're developing. You're not abandoned; you are anchored. And the anchor is not your own strength, your own wisdom, or your own understanding—the anchor is Him. Jesus, the Son of God, the one who speaks to winds and waves, the one who stretches out His hand when you sink, the one who walks on what threatens to take you under.

He is your proof. He is your promise. He is your resolve.

And when you finally see Him—when you finally let the revelation of who He is outweigh the reality of what you're in—that's when you'll discover the secret: you've already made it. You don't have to wait for dry land under your feet. The sign you've arrived is dry land inside your soul. The place called Beautiful isn't just a gate you pass through; it's a revelation you carry. The garden of riches isn't just a land you enter; it's a truth that keeps producing in you.

So lift your head, wipe your eyes, and take heart. You're between miracles, yes—but you're not lost. You're not broken beyond repair. You're not drowning in vain. You are in the hands of the God who takes "later" and turns it into life. And He will finish what He started in you. The boat may not make it. But you will.

Because broken pieces still float.

FINAL THOUGHTS

If you've made it this far, then you've walked with me through storms, wrestled with questions, sat in tension, and maybe even cried some tears you didn't expect to cry. And I need you to know this: the middle is not a punishment, it's a process. It's not God forgetting you; it's God forming you. Every chapter, every story, every moment has been my attempt to show you what I've discovered for myself—that God can handle your raw, and He is faithful to bring you truth.

I can't promise you life will smooth out after this. You will still have transitions. You will still face moments you don't understand. There will still be prayers that seem unanswered, doors that seem closed, and nights when sleep doesn't come easy. But what I can promise you is this: you will never go through any of it alone. And if you can hold on to the revelation of who He is, you will always find resolve, even when you don't find reasons.

Here's the secret to the middle: you don't need to understand it. You just need to understand Him. And if you anchor yourself in who He is, you'll pass every test, you'll survive every storm, and you'll walk into every "later" with peace instead of panic.

So if you're in between miracles right now, don't call it struggling. Call it transition. Call it growth. Call it becoming. You're not failing—you're forming. You're not drifting—you're developing. And sooner than you think, your "later" will arrive. And when it does, you'll look back and say, "I didn't know then what He was doing, but now I understand."

Until then, take courage. Keep walking. Keep believing. Keep surrendering your need to control, to figure it out, to understand it all. And rest in the truth that your Father has already marked your finish before you ever started your journey.

The boat may not make it, but you will. Because broken pieces still float. And you're proof of that. So as you leave these pages and step back into the rhythm of your own middle, I want to leave you with one last declaration. Say it out loud. Let it settle in your spirit. Let it anchor your heart every time doubt, fear, or confusion tries to rise up.

I AM RESOLVED THAT YOU HAVE NO ILL WILL TOWARDS ME... I KNOW YOU WANT ME TO WIN, I KNOW YOU WANT ME TO LIVE!!!

~ JOSH

WHAT A GOD WE HAVE! AND HOW FORTUNATE WE ARE TO HAVE HIM, THIS FATHER OF OUR MASTER JESUS! BECAUSE JESUS WAS RAISED FROM THE DEAD, WE'VE BEEN GIVEN A BRAND-NEW LIFE AND HAVE EVERYTHING TO LIVE FOR, INCLUDING A FUTURE IN HEAVEN—AND THE FUTURE STARTS NOW! GOD IS KEEPING CAREFUL WATCH OVER US AND THE FUTURE. THE DAY IS COMING WHEN YOU'LL HAVE IT ALL—LIFE HEALED AND WHOLE.

I KNOW HOW GREAT THIS MAKES YOU FEEL, EVEN THOUGH YOU HAVE TO PUT UP WITH EVERY KIND OF AGGRAVATION IN THE MEANTIME. PURE GOLD PUT IN THE FIRE COMES OUT OF IT PROVED PURE; GENUINE FAITH PUT THROUGH THIS SUFFERING COMES OUT PROVED GENUINE. WHEN JESUS WRAPS THIS ALL UP, IT'S YOUR FAITH, NOT YOUR GOLD, THAT GOD WILL HAVE ON DISPLAY AS EVIDENCE OF HIS VICTORY.

YOU NEVER SAW HIM, YET YOU LOVE HIM. YOU STILL DON'T SEE HIM, YET YOU TRUST HIM—WITH LAUGHTER AND SINGING. BECAUSE YOU KEPT ON BELIEVING, YOU'LL GET WHAT YOU'RE LOOKING FORWARD TO: TOTAL SALVATION.

1 PETER 1:3-9 (MSG)

ACKNOWLEDGMENTS

Yooooo. Let me be extremely honest—this book was hard to write. Not because I didn't have anything to say, but because of the weight of what I needed to say. I had to fight through thoughts of inadequacy, through questions of whether I still had the goods. This is the longest I've ever spent on a book, not because of the subject matter, but because of the stretching it required of me.

First, I want to say a huge thank you to BEST—Kevin (@iamwilljohnson). I'm so grateful to God for placing you in my life. You give me the freedom and space to just laugh. You pour into me, challenge me, check me, and even rebuke me—all because you love me. I'll never forget that birthday when you picked up the phone, heard something off in my voice, and instead of leaving it there, you hopped in your car, drove 6–8 hours, and showed up at my front door. You'll never know how much that did for me.

To who I call "The Nucleus"—thank you for always being there. From the moment you found out about my grandma, to right now, you've consistently shown me love through your presence. You've offered me a safe space to release my raw feelings without holding anything back, without ever questioning my faith. You've let me be undone, but never dishonored or disrespected my ministry. That's rare, and I don't take it for granted.

To everyone who took the time to contribute to this book—those who were willing to write letters—thank you. Thank you for your boldness, your honesty, and for trusting me with your words. I love y'all real bad. My prayer is that everything good from God be yours.

And finally, to any and everyone who pushed me, held me accountable, encouraged me, sowed seeds, and refused to let me quit—thank you. I couldn't have done this without you.

Other Titles by Joshua D. Blocker

Sins of a Mother
Sins of a Mother II
While in the Desert: 21 Day Devotional
Destiny in Pieces
I Am NOT What They Say: Boy Edition
I Am NOT What They Say: Girl Edition
Dear God: 30 Day Guided Journal

ABOUT THE AUTHOR

Joshua D. Blocker, also known as JoshDaWay, is a dynamic force in entertainment. An award-winning actor, author, screenwriter, director, and founder of DAWAY ENTERTAINMENT, Joshua is renowned for his comedic spontaneity, intelligence, and wide-ranging influence. Hailing from Texas, he holds a Bachelor of Fine Arts from Texas State University and is represented by Cachet Talent Agency. With a passion for storytelling and a commitment to changing lives, Joshua's luminous talent is destined to leave an indelible mark on the industry. Keep an eye on this multifaceted mogul-in-the-making; his journey to greatness is just beginning, and missing out on his work would be a regrettable oversight.

www.ingramcontent.com/pod-product-compliance
Lightning Source LLC
Chambersburg PA
CBHW072002070526
44583CB00015B/1289